NEW DIRECTIONS 26

N D

New Directions in Prose and Poetry 26

Edited by J. Laughlin

with Peter Glassgold and Frederick R. Martin

 A New Directions Book

ACKNOWLEDGMENTS

Grateful acknowledgment is made to the editors and publishers of books
and magazines where some of the selections in this book first appeared:
for Horst Bienek, *The London Magazine*; for Naomi Burton, *Church
World*; for Robert Nichols, *7th Street Anthology* and *City Lights Anthol-
ogy*; for Omar Pound, Agenda Editions, London (Copyright © 1972 by
Omär S. Pound); for Tony Tanner, *Partisan Review* (Copyright © 1972
by Partisan Review).

"Mother Earth," Copyright © 1972 by Gary Snyder

Manufactured in the United States of America
First published clothbound (ISBN: 0–8112–0476–6) and as
New Directions Paperbook 353 (ISBN: 0–8112–0477–4) in 1972
Published simultaneously in Canada by McClelland & Stewart, Ltd.

New Directions Books are published fqr James Laughlin
by New Directions Publishing Corporation,
333 Sixth Avenue, New York 10014

In memoriam
EZRA POUND
1885–1972

CONTENTS

MOTHER EARTH

GARY SNYDER

No one came to the 1972 U.N. Conference on the Environment to give anything—they all came to take. Not to save the planet, but to argue about how to divide it up and stretch it out—how to prolong the agony. People thought and spoke in terms of political divisions and human needs. No one spoke for the actual biological and ethnic zones of the planet, and the interrelated needs of all beings. Except the Hopi Indian delegation from the Southwest. But it was a start.

An owl winks in the shadows.
A lizard lifts on tiptoe, breathing hard.
Young male sparrow stretches up his neck,
    big head, watching—

The Masses are working in the sun. Turn it green.
Turn it sweet. That we may eat.
Grow our meat.

Brazil says "sovereign use of Natural Resource."
Natural? 30,000 kinds of unknown plants,
The living actual people of the jungle—
    sold and tortured—
And a robot in a suit who speaks for a delusion called "Brazil"
    can speak for *them*?

The whales turn and glisten, plunge
        and sound and rise again,
Hanging over subtly darkening deeps,
Flowing like breathing planets
        in the sparkling whorls of
        living light—

And Japan quibbles for words on
        who can they kill?
A once-great Buddhist nation
        dribbles mercury
        like gonorrhea
        in the sea

Père David's Deer, the Elaphure,
Lived in the tule marshes of the Yellow River
Two thousand years ago—and lost its home to rice—
The Forests of Loyang were logged and all the silt and
Sand flowed down, and gone, by
        1200 A.D.

Wild geese hatched out in Siberia
        head south over basins of the Yang, the Huang,
        what we call "China"
On flyways they have used ten thousand years—
Ah, China, where are the Tigers, the wild boars,
        the monkeys,
        like the snows of yesteryear?
Gone in a mist, a flash, and the dry hard ground
Is parking space for 50,000 trucks.
Is man most precious of all things?
—Then let us love him, and his brothers, all those
Fading living beings—

The U.S. runs a lawnmower in Vietnam,
Chopping up trees and ricefields—bits of people—
Farmer's leg or arm—babies broken up and mixed—

North America, Turtle Island, taken by invaders
        who wage war around the world.

May ants, may bees, may fireflies,
Starfish, abalone, otters, wolves and elk—
Rise! and pull away their giving flow from
    all the robot nations.

SOLIDARITY! The People!
Standing Tree People!
Flying Bird People!
Swimming Sea People!
Four-legged, two-legged, people!

How can the head-heavy power-hungry politic-scientist
Government two-world Capitalist-Imperialist
Third-world Communist paper-shuffling male
    non-farmer jet-set bureaucrats
Speak for the green of the leaf? Speak for the soil?
    Speak for Man?

(Ah Margaret Mead . . . do you sometimes dream of Samoa?)

The robots argue how to parcel out our Mother Earth
To last a little longer,
    like vultures flapping
Belching, gurgling
    near a dying Doe.

An owl winks in the shadow,
A lizard lifts on tiptoe
    breathing hard.
The whales turn and glisten,
    plunge and
    sound, and rise again,
Flowing like breathing planets
In sparkling whorls
Of living light.

FIVE POEMS

KENNETH REXROTH

THE FAMILY

Late night
Coming back to Melbourne
From a party on the Kangaroo Plains,
We stop the car by a black pool.
The air is immobile, crystalline.
I get out, light a match,
And study my star map.
I blow out the match,
And overhead, and before and below me
Doubled in the unmoving water,
The million stars come on
That I have never seen before,
And will never see again.
And there are the two
Daughter universes of my universe,
The Magellanic Clouds—
Two phosphorescent amoebas overhead,
And two in the bottomless water.

VOID ONLY

Time like glass
Space like glass
I sit quiet
Anywhere Anything
Happens
Quiet loud still turbulent
The serpent coils
On itself
All things are translucent
Then transparent
Then gone
Only emptiness
No limits
Only the infinitely faint
Song
Of the coiling mind
Only

NO WORD

The trees hang silent
In the heat . . . . .

                    Undo your heart
                    Tell me your thoughts
                    What you were
                    And what you are . . . . .

                              Like bells no one
                              Has ever rung.

SUCHNESS

In the theosophy of light,
The logical universal
Ceases to be anything more
Than the dead body of an angel.
What is substance? Our substance
Is whatever we feed our angel.
The perfect incense for worship
Is camphor, whose flames leave no ashes.

IT IS A GERMAN HONEYMOON

They are stalking humming birds
The jewels of the new world
The rufous hummingbird dives
Along his parabola
Of pure ether. We forgot—
An imponderable and
Invisible elastic
Crystal is the womb of space.
They wait with poised cameras
Focused telescopic lens
Beyond the crimson trumpet vine.
He returns squealing against
The sky deeper than six billion
Light years, and plunges through sun
Blaze to the blood redflower womb.
A whirling note in the lens of space.
"Birds are devas" says Morris
Graves. "They live in a world
without Karma." No grasping,
No consequence, only the
Grace of the vectors that form
The lattices of the unending
Imponderable crystal.

The blond and handsome young man
And woman are happy, they
Love each other, when they have
gone around the world they will
Sit in the Grunewald and
Look at a picture of a
California hummingbird.
Nobody can swim across
The Great River. Turn your back
And study the spotted wall.
Turn around on the farther shore.
Nine dice roll out, one by one.
The mouse eats them. They never were.
The hundred flowers put their
Heads together, yellow stamens and
Swelling pistils. Between them
In midspace they generate
A single seed. You cannot
Find it in a telescope.
Found, you could not see it in
An electron microscope.

PARTEI

YUMIKO KURAHASHI

Translated by Samuel Grolmes and Yumiko Tsumura

One day you asked if I had made up my mind yet. I knew that you had wanted to bring it up any number of times even before then. And besides you were unusually direct. So I felt that I should show a certain frankness too. I answered, I have. You began explaining, To enter the Party means that you subordinate your entire private life, problems of love included, of course, to the rules of the Party. You kept your glasses too well polished, I could not see the expression in your naked eyes behind the glare. The clattering of your teeth made me feel I was looking at the occlusion of some malformed skeleton, you must have been abnormally excited. Without thinking I let out a muffled animal-like laugh. And you took my hand in yours. As always it was warm and damp. I think it is a slightly repulsive sensation. You seemed to be trying to make sure that I had made up my mind. So I had to reassure you in words that required exaggerated gestures.

You mentioned in sequence a number of procedures I would have to follow to get formal approval to enter the Party. To tell the truth I was not listening to most of it. The enthusiasm you displayed over this kind of clerical matter was comical to me. Drawing up the Personal History, you said, is the peak of the procedures. You said that in your own case the Personal History came out like this and sat a fat bundle of documents in front of me. There it was, in front of me as if something had accumulated in a large heap.

8

The way the papers were thumb soiled and worn seemed to guarantee authoritative certainty of its having passed through a severe screening inside the Party. I am suffocated with shame at the thought of your life being handled by so many other people—it makes no difference to me that it goes by the name System. Perhaps your face is a thing like a red birthmark of Belief. And if it had not spread over even your eyes, I think you too could recognize what a comical thing your Personal History is.

We were inside some room. It was a filthy room, walls starting to crack, in the depths of a maze inside an absurd huge building. Since the first time you brought me to this room I sensed that in some curious way I had been made into an abstraction. I rarely laughed anymore, I spoke with fixed logic, the few times I did laugh it was with fixed vigor. There was no sadness, it would have been entirely silly in that building. In fact, the moment one stepped into this Dormitory, as the building was called, Reality was transformed into a world of foul-smelling mucilage, and in spite of the thick walls which separated the space into rooms of various sizes, the rooms combined, the walls were bandages, the whole impression something like a cohesion of cells stuffed with oppressive air. That time too I had stepped into one of those cells and ignoring the Students who were going about their individual tasks I was having a talk with you. Once when I was telling you my impression of this room I had said, The air is abnormal, too thick, yet somehow abstract. But after asking a few questions you dismissed my impression.

You said that in short I do not have enough experience in Party work. You thought that was what was responsible for my lack of self-confidence. You said it to console me. And I too said, In fact the best solution seems to be to get used to it. Nevertheless, I cannot get used to this room so easily. There seem to be too many people, the dust and the noise they raise, and even more that especially foul odor from the lower half of the body that group living produces, irritate me. It had been bothering me for some time before that that there were snips from the Military Rescript scribbled all over the walls and ceiling. Don't you think this sort of thing is out of place in a Dormitory? I reproached. Now and then some Student living in the room would bellow out the Party song. And then other songs of that sort would start to erupt from the scattered rooms those walls separated. I believe it is an environment I could never get used to.

I can say that until about that time I had loved you almost totally. I am not sure how to define Total, but you always made me feel that it was Total. From the first time you met me, you had shown interest in me, and I had shown more than a little interest in you too. After a while I said I love you and you accepted it. At that time your tears were lavish. You insisted that it was I, the fact of my love, that made you, a member of the Party, secrete such human tears. It made me feel a little proud at the moment. But when I really think about it it is absolutely illogical. First, it is ridiculous that you are moved by the correspondence between the Party and something human. After that, at your suggestion, we announced to our Comrade Students that we had decided to love each other, and we received their congratulations. I turned crimson with humiliation. Nevertheless, I think the fact that I loved you a relatively long time, and above all I believed that I did, was for no other reason than that I was inside those abstract walls. If we had been in a place with lighter air, if we had shared those festive trivia of everyday life, it probably would not have turned out this way.

Incidentally, to write out my Personal History so thoroughly as to include even that sort of thing was an extremely difficult job for me. Because I am the sort of person who feels almost no interest in my own past. You advised me to build on one sinew of logic, to select details from my past as scrupulously as possible, to summarize and unify, to lick it over with my tongue at times, and bind it all to my motive for entering the Party. When I was born, both of my parents died, I was poor, I was betrayed, I had learned the contradictions of the world through my skin. And for these reasons I not only had sufficient motive to enter the Party but also through various experiences in my past my character was polished to be a member of the Party. You explained I should write it out like this.

And then, a few days later I told you, It looks like I won't be able to write my Personal History. You began again by reproducing my past from infancy and argued eloquently that my entering the Party at present was an Inevitability. There was something amazing about your tenacity and I cannot deny that I admired and was a little attracted by the fact that my own past could be so finely colored. But I finally interrupted you. The problem is not that sort of thing, I said. No matter how much you try to brush and crease my past, I cannot say, Therefore I Must Enter the Party. I feel *honte* to restrain and defend myself according to my past. I think I want to escape from the past, throw my body into the future. I chose the Party and made up my mind to restrict my freedom according to the Party. There is no reason attached to it, nor did any cause-and-effect relationship whatsoever lead to my determination. Isn't it sufficient my determination be accepted by the Party? But you objected. According to you it was a dangerous thought. You repeatedly warned me, For any individual to enter the Party an objective Inevitability that the Party can accept is necessary.

I left the Dormitory feeling a little disappointment. Then I rode the train almost two hours to get back to my own room, and just slept. About the time the morning light threw an orange-colored hope over things, I put on my sweat-soaked clothes just as they were and left to go back to the Dormitory again. I was quite diligent at my work. That day too I was paired with you to go to K City to visit two or three Unions. Of course I would rather have been paired with a different Student, but since it had been decided that way there was nothing I could do.

We arrived in K City about two. Thin rays of sun pierced the clouded sky, it was muggy. When I looked down as we crossed the land bridge I saw the massive junctions of freight tracks spreading out radially, being drawn into the numerous Factories. The fact that the streets are narrow, forming shelves pushing out into the sea, and the Factories made of patches of black iron plate are built up in heaps one on top of the other, makes it all resemble an ungainly but imposing statue when I look at it as a whole. You transferred from train to train and climbed up and down those iron ladders. The Factories had originally been constructed in irregularly divided lots, and as a result of additions having been made not only on the side but top and bottom as well they often invaded the lots of other Factories and sometimes were even leaning over other Factories. So we often got confused and stepped into a Factory we were not in charge of. Even when we found the right Factory it was still difficult to get exactly to the Union. The guard would ask us our names and what our jobs were, and then we always had to think up false names. It was absurd that he should ask our names at this point, but he was always satisfied with what we told him and gave us passes. Once we got into the Factory we still had difficulty till we discovered the location of the Union. Sometimes the Union was not inside the Factory, sometimes it would be in a barracks beside a trash dump exposed to the salt wind from the sea. But in most cases the Union was attached to some gloomy Factory building and the Union Men who lived there looked at us from the darkness with their eyes gleaming yellow. I thought they were exactly like owls, but you were offended by the metaphor. Actually they were gentlemanly and it was true that they did not give me the impression of being Laborers. Our mission was to explain things about the Labor School that was going to open soon, and to promote it, and at the same time to feel out the present condition of the Union. You smiled all through it and made yourself amiable to the Union Men who appeared. I could not. But as we were leaving the Factory you said that you did not have complete trust in the Union members either. No matter what the situation we should not lose our sense of class precaution. That is, they may be Union members and they may not. They may not even be Laborers. The actual situation is always entangled in complications, and we have only our practical experience as touchstone to distinguish those who are genuine Laborers from those who are not, you said. Of course, to me it was incomprehensible, and also impossible.

I should mention the circle to which I belonged. It was one of the circles which had been given the general name of Settlement. Ours was called the Labor School Settlement and was to work mainly by getting in among the Laborers in K City. We called the Students who were doing the same work Comrades. It seems to me the name is a little damp. Hot, and a little sweaty like your hand. When I utter the word Comrades I almost have a feeling that I belong to a group of some sort that advocates fellowship under God. Yet what was disturbing to me was the relation between the Comrades of this Labor School and the Party. Of course it was certain that there were some Party members among the Comrades. But I couldn't tell which they were. The Comrades without exception pretended to be Party members and I can say in fact that all of them were hoping to enter the Party. Yet in formal situations all of them behave as if they were not Party members. I think that is to give an external appearance for the outside world that would make even ordinary Students feel it was easy to participate in the Labor School. The members of the Party that I knew were you and S. S was a big man in the Party Area Committee, the expression in his eyes that stung my skin like a snake and his professional eloquence were enough to convince me of that. It seems S had been infatuated with me for some time.

When the Labor School opened you often pressed me about the Personal History, and urged me to finish it quickly. I can't write it so easily, I said. And you said, Why? I was annoyed and answered, It's just as I always tell you. And you criticized me for being irresolute and excessively conscience-ridden. And then all at once you brought up the M Incident. Innocent Comrades were sentenced to death in a courthouse surrounded by armed police and armored cars, you said, trying to kindle my sense of justice. I was compelled to say, I can understand the injustice of it very well, however I regret that I cannot have any great interest in it. I said, What does interest me now is the problem of my entering the Party. I think I am in agreement with you on that point. And I want to comprehend that in a state of distinct consciousness so that even if the M Incident infuriates me I cannot make that my motive for entering the Party. I cannot avoid feeling *honte* in the face of opaqueness.

We started organizing a private, small-scale Study Circle utilizing the Laborers we became acquainted with at the Labor School as a hold. And so around that time my work first was concerned with the management of the Labor School, especially negotiating with the instructors of the school, and secondly to work as a tutor in this Study Circle, and thirdly to walk around investigating the developments in the Union. I quickly grew intimate with the Laborers in the Study Circle. They had thick-jointed limbs, they walked bandy legged, their skin was dark and hot. They talked of nothing but concrete things, to me it was excessively concrete, to a degree that I felt faint. I was conducting the Study Circle in an attic that jutted out over the sea at the top of a narrow emergency ladder at a bookstore.

One day in town I met a Laborer who always attended the Study Circle, he treated me to food. The Laborer was better dressed than I and he seemed to have money, so I thanked him, but felt a little embarrassed. The Laborer and I climbed up to the bookstore attic and waited, but that day no one else came. The Laborer said, This kind of thing happens so often, and for some time the two of us sat there holding our knees. It was hot. I was the one who said, We should take off our clothes, and the Laborer agreed. Outside the window the sea was rolling brown waves, it disgorged a stench of kerosene, metal, and a variety of organic substances. The Factory smoke clouded the sky red, and the evening sun stood still forming one ripened-persimmon spot in the smoke. When I looked at the Laborer's skin, it was tinged red like pig iron, I began to feel the same kind of interest in the Laborer that I might feel for some unknown animal.

As for the incident which followed, there is hardly anything to tell. I somehow touched the Laborer's body and found it was made of hard muscle. He was surprised. His interest in me aroused, he immediately forced me open and went about being loved by me, pouring his hot breath over me. It was more unpleasant than painful, I was pushed completely open. Even though the Laborer was inside me he was as alien as ever, and I was annoyed by this distance, as if two animals of different species happened to meet and just have intercourse on the spot. But I went on, almost completely clearheaded. I was even generous to the Laborer. If he wanted it I could submit anytime after this, I think I wanted it too. The Laborer was clean in spite of his appearance. But terribly hard, heavy, awkward to deal with, without language, and his Reality was nothing but that simple concrete life. Since then the hope that I may sometime be able to understand Laborers began to nourish my days.

I asked your opinion of this hope. That's good! you said promptly, I should make more positive efforts to understand Laborers you said, and offered S as an example of a Comrade who combined in himself the qualities of both Laborer and Student. S is a Student and at the same time a Laborer, you said. But I refuted that, S is neither. His filthy weirdness that smacks of something amphibian comes from that, I said and left to locate and negotiate with a temporary instructor for the Labor School. The residence of one candidate was in a place difficult to find in the midst of a concentration of houses. I know through some sort of connection A, for example I meet with him and request that he take the position of instructor. A says he is sorry but he is not available at that time on that day, and introduces me to B as a suitable person. When I finally locate B and request the same thing of him, B declines in the same way and refers me to C. The series is winding and stretches on endlessly, so for several days I had the job of reeling in the sweet-potato vines of Progressive-Cultured-Man which were being reeled out this way. I have to add that I never built up any presumptuous hope. They were busy, and since the instructor's pay at the Labor School was poor, I think their shy refusals were appropriate.

I tirelessly explained the significance and the present condition of the Labor School and they listened with enthusiastic faces. Both of us were enthusiastic, more about feigning enthusiasm, and did not necessarily believe it all. They seemed to be afraid of something, and I had to go on swallowing that vinegar sensation, behaving like a missionary. But I finally came across a Progressive Poet with spare time and had him undertake the job of instructor.

He came punctually on the appointed day, but another Poet that I did not know also showed up to be an instructor. I heard that a Comrade who had been reeling in sweet-potato vines separately had gone out and found this other Poet. I was befuddled and divided the pay in two and had them both lecture at the same time. They snuggled up like a pair of birds and talked alternately regarding the Shop Literary Circle.

I remember that I was severely criticized afterward by S for this matter. He said I lacked ability to carry out anything, and then suddenly asked what had become of the Personal History that I was supposed to submit to the Party. I kept silent. All the time he stared at me as if I were a Thing, and I felt nervous because he made no attempt to hide his own desire. To draw me out, he said he would help me write it himself. Of course, I refused. Then S attacked your Opportunist Attitude by telling me that I was as timid and wishy-washy as a rabbit and that you were as much to blame as I was.

About the time the rainy season began, I finally finished the Personal History and came to your room to show it to you. I had simply jotted down the facts in the order of their occurrence. Even so, it went into fairly minute detail and was bulky enough not to suffer in comparison with your Personal History. You read it nodding at every word. It is really an irritating habit. I was disgusted. Particles of water the rain produced filled the room and stirred up the usual foul odor all the more. But by that time I seemed to be getting a little used to this kind of environment, so while you were indulging yourself in reading, I cheerfully walked around the room and conversed with the other Students about Revolution. Speaking of the vital Revolution, you suddenly interrupted, what you pointed out was that judging from my Personal History my own grasp of the Inevitability of Revolution seemed insufficient. I blew up. Don't talk in such a stupid way, I told you. Revolution is not anything that exists outside me. If you say it is how can the Inevitability of something external to me influence my freedom, my choice? It isn't because Revolution is Inevitable that I enter the Party, it is because I wish to choose Revolution that I enter. And I choose to become all the more free by restricting my own freedom. I said, My participation makes Revolution an inevitable thing for me. You grabbed up my words and tossed them away one by one, you cut off my argument with your hard glassy eyes and the cigarette smoke that you exhaled incessantly. Almost simultaneously we both screamed, Why can't you understand!

With this crack of discord left unmended, you as a formal representative of the Party accepted my Personal History and on your own became my Recommender, acting as my agent in all the procedures inside the Party Cell. My Personal History will probably pass through the hands of one person after another, getting smeared with saliva and thumbed dirty, getting worn thin till gradually it is pushed up to the superior official. As it is taken further away from me it ceases to be mine, and will probably be treated as one solid substance. When I thought of that I became happy, and at the same time worried. I thought by all means I wanted to see the screening process. It probably resembles the process of a vending machine, for example, eating up a coin, swallowing automatically, moving intricately, and admirably vomiting out one passenger ticket.

One day when the world was being scorched white by the strong August sun, I felt nausea a few times during the morning. When the Labor School finished and the Laborers had gone home, I was terribly tired. But I went over to S's boardinghouse and arranged things for two or three days and cleared up some of the remaining business. At that time S asked me if I was going back to the Dormitory. When I answered that it depended on how well the work progresses, he laughed as if he were satisfied. I added that in fact I was completely exhausted and thought it would be a fairly heavy strain on me to go back from K City. S looked down my body with eyes yellowed from constant fatigue that are characteristic of people who are always Busy, and asked if something was wrong with me lately. The question was appropriate. Since the lower part of my body had begun to swell a little conspicuously, and considering the nausea I was frequently feeling and the dropsi-

cal swelling in my legs, I readily admitted that it was due to preg-
nancy. Who is he? S asked, I don't know, I answered. I added,
Perhaps a Laborer. I choked and made an ugly face turning my
eyes up and down trying to swallow the shame. And I explained
stammering, But it wasn't so often. This seemed to stimulate S all
the more. He pushed me into the littered books and in his eagerness
to take me said that since things had come this far it did not make
any difference . . . Afterward S showed me several remedies, but for
some reason I did not have much interest and went on enduring the
nausea in silence. Aside from that, I questioned, what has become
of my Personal History. With a vague smile playing about his lips
he tried to evade me. Even I can't tell you that, he said, and then
said, But a Party Membership Card will probably come down soon.

For several days after that with a deepening sense of *honte*, I was
sweaty even when I kept still, and I felt that the world was reeling.
My head collided with a phlegmatic abstract wall and was scraped
against it. I knew that in fact it was I myself that seemed to be the
wall. I was closed up in a wall of the past that I had chosen myself,
and was about to be asphyxiated in the heat. I think this vapid state
is comical. I could probably affix the name Farce to it. But there
were times when I broke through the wall and protruded into the
outside world, the lightness of the air there surprised me.

About that time, several new Students entered our circle as Set-
tlers. At your suggestion we decided to hold a one-week training
camp beside the M River in K City. At first I was more or less
interested in this training camp, but that was because group life,
which was composed of a regulated progress of daily life from
eating to evacuating, reminded me of Military Life. Generally, I
think, group life results in an insensitivity to *honte* itself, a familiar-
ity with that foul smell human beings have. And this training-camp
life was the same. All around me, with you especially as the leading
figure, things like frankness, friendship, mutual love—what the
others like to call Mutual Consciousness, to me a feeling of embar-
rassment—continued to be secreted. Sometimes I saw them—myself
included—as a pack of dogs bound together with a rope of *honte*.

When we gathered at night on the riverbank, it was actually like
a garden party, and the Comrades were beginning to pair off into a
number of love-couples during the salon-sweet conversation. I tried
to speak to you of this *honte*, even with you clasping my hand and
the annoying lukewarm river breeze and night bugs swarming

around me, but it was futile. The others were going crazy singing songs and trampling the wet grass under their dance. And then when we returned to the lodge and the routine all-night talk about each person's History began, it came around to my turn after a number of other Students. I said, There is nothing in my past to talk about. Then, you urged me, showing a zealous generosity, in that case go into the problem you are most interested in at present. As soon as I mentioned the word Party, their faces all turned to metal masks, and their vacant focusless eyes looked into space, trying vainly to cling together. I suppose it was wrong to mention the word Party in the tone I used. You kept winking at me. I blew up. And abruptly pointed out, The two-faced attitude of this circle is disgusting. I thought at this time the relationship between the Party and us should be made clear. But this is a difficult problem, you said, trying to put it off. I held on tenaciously. A large number of Students have come in. They have become Comrades, have found something to live for, have expended tremendous energy, but it all resembles a sport, a way to make the Student days enjoyable. And the aspirations and the inferiority complex they have toward the Party leaves a muddy residue on the surface of contact between the Party and this circle . . . I think I talked with more coherent logic, but my memory of it isn't clear. I remember only that someone criticized me for being Sectarian.

Paying no attention, I went on, I still haven't understood the significance of this kind of activity myself, and when I try to consider at what point my participation touches Reality, I feel almost like I'm going insane, I said. As a matter of fact right now, and with no hope whatsoever, I am doing nothing more than scratching the icy sky trying to leave behind a streak of light in the darkness where there are no stars. As for the possibility of such a streak developing to the point of Revolution, I hold no Belief whatever. The only thing I can believe is that to the extent the system restricts my freedom, I am freer than I have ever been.

When the air cooled as night came, the afternoon sweat began to form salt on our earth-colored skin. The Comrades seemed to be sleepy. It made their faces almost entirely symbolic. The white beads of sweat on their cheeks were like decorative stars on earthen figures . . . And also the constant sound of their slapping themselves against the unrelenting attack of the mosquitoes was adding a mystic Ritualistic mood to this meeting. I thought this was a perfectly Esoteric Ritual. What is important now is not a matter of understanding, but rather a matter of being receptive to a form which creates understanding. Actually no one understood what I was talking about. Of course I admit that I did not expect anything. Finally, you began a calm Criticism of me, your glasses were glittering. You were slightly diffident, but you set about providing for me with the term *Petit Bourgeois*. I was full of anger from the neck up, and turned crimson. I was used to being stared at by others, being clothed in other's words, but in this case I could not be patient. This handy garment *Petit Bourgeois* was just too comical. I was deprived of words. So you assumed that I was submitting to your criticism and you began to speak lucidly. We participate in a circle called the Labor School so that we can develop understanding with the Laborers, draw in living energy from their Reality, and through this work we can bind ourselves together in human affection as Comrades and we can escape loneliness and isolation. . . . I was intrigued by your summation. That was really skillful, perfect, I told you. But I believe it is a way of thinking I cannot understand. You seem very cautiously to omit Revolution and merely advocate unprincipled Service and Fraternity, what of this? But when I saw that no one was speaking anymore it might have been that the earthen figures had fallen into a soil-like sleep. They were all snuggling their sweat-chilled bodies together, hugging their knees or sticking out their filthy barefoot soles.

At dawn we separated into several groups and went out for Labor Union Inspection. I was paired with you to visit the S Petroleum company. There a Laborer at the Public Information Section began to talk to me eagerly as soon as he saw me. I thought I remembered having seen the Laborer but it is not important. I tried to leave at once but he chased me as far as the restricted area of the raw Petroleum tanks, he told me he could not forget me. I questioned him in detail to understand what relation he had with me, and he insisted that he was one of the Laborers who had attended the Study Circle and that he had had intercourse with me. He said he wanted to marry me. I said something curt in refusal. I could not understand very well what he was talking about, something about wanting to set up home completely embarrassed me. I want children, he said. And I told him, I am capable of having the child but I have no intention of doing so. I am thinking of disposing of it. You were waiting for me outside the gate and asked if I had been Maneuvering the Laborer. The very thought of it made me laugh. Still you kept insisting eagerly that I should draw the Laborer close to the Party.

The next day you caught me in the washroom of the lodge and said you wanted me to come with you. You explained that a directive regarding some mission had come from the Party. We dropped by the Dormitory to remove everything from our bodies that would reveal our identity. Then we went to stand at the entrance of the gaudy shop-lined street in front of N station to sell the Party Newspaper. The election and the Nuclear Disarmament Conference were imminent, you explained. It was a propaganda movement in connection with that. Following your example, I cried out from time to time, but it sounded hollow, and I tried to scream *agitation* but my voice was beginning to crack. It did not go well. We did not sell a single copy of the Party newspaper and they were soon yellowed and curled by the strong sunlight. But you kept an intensely firm attitude and did not even try to wipe off the sweat that was pouring down you.

A little after noon we were arrested. The Police explained there was a question as to whether our actions were in violation of the Election and the Road and Traffic Control laws and in polite language requested us to come to the police station. We followed, dragging our apple crate behind us and hugging the Party newspapers under our arms. You urged me to try to escape. But I did not. The room we were put in was built of crude planking and it struck me as being meager, like a janitor's quarters. You kept silent, and I was silent too. A few Police surrounded us and set about interrogating us, mainly about the Party. The interrogation was somewhat boring. That is to say, it started with names and addresses, then such formalities as our status, and developed into leading questions which were mixed with mistaken conjectures about the Party, and when it met our silence it returned again to names and addresses. During this purely repetitive interrogation which was like listening to a monotonous symphony, I could indulge freely in my own thoughts. It was not even necessary to give a false name here. I was a completely nameless suspect, and although I was connected with some System, I was one glassy particle without any characteristics, all strings and appendages cut off and thrown away. The Police received our attitude as something expected and said they wanted to take our fingerprints. What do you want fingerprints for, you asked. The Police glanced at each other and grinned. It must have been something they themselves did not understand. I thought this sort of thing was terribly clumsy and unnecessary so I clenched my hand into a fist. Then the Police lifted me onto a table locking my joints in their arms, and worked a screwdriver under my fingers to open them. Eventually they got the edge of the screwdriver into the flesh under my nails and pried my fingers open one by one. I began to enjoy resisting and the Police seemed to feel the same. They went about the business smilingly and then they locked us in a room that resembled a toilet.

About dark a huge man brought in some food. To stimulate your appetite you did a few arm and leg exercises, and then began to eat with your face right down in the aluminum tray. You pressed food on me while you were eating and said, We will probably be released in the morning. I said, I don't particularly hope so, but it may be unavoidable. You were a little surprised. But suddenly you took my hand affectionately in yours. You paid me an exaggerated compliment for not betraying the Party in spite of all sorts of torture, and for the first time you called me Fellow Comrade. You assured me, You must be a person who truly loves the Party. No, I'm not such a person, I said, and cut the talk off simply by saying, It is impossible to betray anything in a situation like this. Even so, the words Fellow Comrade gave me the feeling of being shut up in an extremely repulsive container. I said, I definitely want you to stop calling me that, and told you, I have made up my mind not to enter the Party. That was the first time I noticed what an awful squint you have. I was convulsed with laughter and got a cramp in my stomach. What have you been doing all this time? You are an absolute farce, I said rolling over and over on the floor. I laughed until I vomited.

You were completely baffled, but when I finally stopped vomiting and confessed the fact of my pregnancy, my eyes still filled with tears, you were staring at me, your pupils drawn into the center of your face. Then you removed your glasses and began to cry. There's not much I can say, I told you, I don't love you and I never loved the Laborer or S or the Party. When I finished, I was alone. Your sobbing and the smell of my own excreta hardly disturbed me. I think I was exceptionally clearheaded. But I prevented my clearheadedness from going toward an analysis of things and the establishment of a cause-and-effect relationship. I should strip off all reason attached to my actions, I should amputate all meaning attached to the data that cling to them so sluggishly. I should not have written the Personal History and I have to retrieve it quickly. That was my first *honte*, but I should not pile *honte* upon *honte* to try to efface it. Somewhere, the Party does exist, and it works through some strangely complicated mechanism, it must be swallowing up and vomiting out individuals like me in its ceaseless expanding and contracting. But its existence must be very abstract. And the fact that it is composed of a whole of various Decrees and Esoteric Rituals makes it appear to me to be the same as some type of religious sect. Its purpose is Salvation and salvation is to believe. But I do not believe in anything. I did not believe in the Inevitability of Revolution and I did not believe in the objective significance of my actions. I simply decided to choose the Party, and I remember it was done with no Belief.

Perhaps this rule will hold for the things I choose from now on. I immediately fell off to sleep and when I woke up it was unexpectedly light in the cell in the police station. You were exhausted and slept on. The coarse flesh of your cheeks, the fat neck, the glasses, they were all there independently. They have no meaning to me now whatever.

After a while we were given some food. When we had had our evacuation, we were taken to the Police Chief's office and following a brief interrogation—it was almost a repetition of the one of the previous day—we were released. You threatened to demand a written apology, but the Police Chief explained that it would be an impossibility for the authorities to make a public apology to a nameless nondescript.

Stirring up some kind of hope again, you went to K City to return to the training camp. I returned to my own room for the first time in several months. It welcomed me with such an indifferent air that I hesitated to touch the walls or the furniture for a while. On the desk I found a letter with no return address. Along with a notice to the effect that I had been approved to enter the Party, a red Party Membership Card fell out. I looked at it and after examining it carefully threw it away.

I have made up my mind to start the procedures for leaving the Party.

BOYHOOD IN GLEIWITZ

HORST BIENEK

Translated by Eva Hesse

TRANSLATOR'S NOTE: *Horst Bienek was born in 1930 in the town of Gleiwitz, the German name for Gliwice, in a part of Silesia originally settled by Slavs in the 6th century. Groups of German settlers began arriving five hundred years later, followed in the 12th century by a second wave that came at the invitation of the Polish ruling house of Piast. Yet very few of the inhabitants of Gleiwitz in the 1930s were descendants of these early Polish and German settlers, the vast majority being workers from Germany and Poland who had been drawn to Silesia by the Industrial Revolution.*

Much intermarriage took place between the two ethnic groups, and each has left its mark on the language of the other. This development is pointed up in Bienek's poems, where all the Germans (the Mainkas, Schewczyk, Skowronnek, Sczelski, Piechotta, etc.) have, like himself, Polish names—sometimes with slightly Germanized spelling—and speak German infused with Polish expressions and using a syntax influenced by Polish.

Gleiwitz, which in 1939 had a mixed population of 117,000, today numbers over 125,000 Polish inhabitants, most of whom were born there. The German Silesians fled from Silesia as the Red Army approached. However, all maps of Central Europe printed in West Germany show that the Federal Republic still lays claim to the whole of Silesia as well as other territories which became in-

tegral parts of Poland, the Czechoslovak People's Republic, and the Soviet Union as a result of the last war. These official maps reflect the vague hope of successive West German governments that either political unrest in Eastern Europe or a possible third world war might result in the reconstitution of the Reich within its 1939 borders.

After World War II, Bienek joined Bertolt Brecht's theater group in Berlin but, becoming unwittingly involved with an underground agent in East Berlin, was arrested and sent to Workuta labor camp in Siberia. On being amnestied, Bienek went to West Germany, where he became a successful writer. Among other things, he has made a twenty-minute television film of Ezra Pound, the influence of whose "Pisan Cantos" is to be noted occasionally in "Boyhood in Gleiwitz."

I

Memories of woods in winter
    Pistulka[1] and his merry men
a turbid river turgidly flowing
    a Corpus Christi procession
vinous shouts from the next-door Mainkas
    and on one occasion
        a broadcast interrupted by shots
which prefaced the first thrust eastward[2]

That is all
    a few scenes
        from an overexposed film
sporadic shadows and
    if I peer hard enough
        perhaps a face
           a movement
            a gesture
an anonymous smile

Is boyhood memory
or memory boyhood?
Reading Borges my mind dwells on the unremitting
    memory of Irenlo Fuñes

What interests me in Sartre is his
    relation to Descartes
What went on, I wonder, in Coriolanus' head
    as they made him captive

      Now, of a sudden,
the cracking of an almond
the smell of fish frying in Bunzlau earthenware
a jay squawking in Laband Woods
scenes all a blur
    flicker across the retina

Miners returning homeward
    the roundabout's white horses
        with hempen manes
Father Schewczyk and 12 ministrants
        scurrying to extreme unction
Along the straight road to Königshütte
rowan trees in September,
    their tops shot off by tanks
        and a song entangled in the branches
Ich danze mit Djär innen Himmel chinein . . .[3]
Waltzing with you all the way to heaven . . .

Chocolate obtained for sugar coupons
    a vitamin tablet
        as host of the Third Reich
dissolving slowly on the tongue
Later: clipping out war scenes from the illustrateds
B.I., Erika, Oberschlesischer Wanderer
and Skowronnek, the teacher, insistent:
Nu kläbt mal de Bülder n eijre Häfte
und schraijbt von sägraiche Fäldzück na Poln[4]
So yuh jes' stick dem pitchers in yuh'r copybooks
and write me up thet VIC-toh-rius drive inna PO-lan'

Another wood, another river
    the Klodnitz bore death to Kosel
1944: saw
    my first corpse
        dog-tag around neck

drifting towards Breslau, Cologne or maybe Paradiso
Hoppek, Josel, Alfongs and me
  standing on the bank
   pissing in the reeds
Hoppek, I recall,
  had the biggest pullock[5]
   you dupa[6] you, I've screwed little Hedy . . .
At the same spot later, shots rang out
  as they were driving the stripies[7] from Auschwitz
     some 40 km. off
my gaze fixes on a decorator's cart
high wheels, a broken arm protruding through the spokes
  corpses piled up on the planks
   faces covered over with rags
    feet trussed with wire
this scene—January 19, 1945—etched more deeply than the rest

And deeper still the shooting
  torn-up pictures
   faces obliterated
    the town an inferno
long treks through woods and across streams
shots, endless processions of refugees[8]
it all comes back
as I buy a ticket for the new flick
Lemmy Caution in *Alphaville*

Is boyhood memory
or memory boyhood?
All that remains
  a gesture, a smile, a stroking hand
air raid warnings, a good-night kiss
    once waited for in vain
a room
  filled with emptiness
   made more intense by the night
at 35 scenes tend to linger
  as neuroses

Boyhood is a film
projected upon the retina
    overexposed
peeling an orange
    reading in the paper of a Boeing 7-oh-7
crashing into Fuji
    or composing a rather unconvincing letter
        to the girl friend
    suddenly
in the geometry of the alphabet
    in the fantastic intersection of the lines
        in the explosion of silence
            unleashing nothing but stillness:
the silent relapse into boyhood
    (never a plunge into the void)
deep down at bedrock
    if you look closely
there is always boyhood
if you do not finish the letter
do not read the news to the end
do not go on peeling the orange
you will discover it
    for an instant
        and forever

Each new day lops an hour off boyhood
leave time to the eye
    and to time, waste
the freight yard and the steam
    the engines and the turbid, turgid river
the road to the mine
    the highway to Przeskläbje[9]
    everlasting boyhood
with images emerging from smoke and dreams and the flames

II   ON THE KLODNITZ

The thousand voices from the deep[10]
not like that at all, he said

went down to the river
    arms stemming against the wind
        forcing fleeting doors
our laughter
    cutting rings in the glazed air
    shattered in October
marsh marigolds like fiery tongues
Totschka and Huss[11] burning at the stake
stinging nettles
    lashing against our unruly knees
Wednesday's geography lesson: Oppa   Zinna   Hotzenplotz
    Glatzer Neisse[12]
flinging ourselves down upon the grass
    tearing at the bracken
with our teeth
summer that year had a taste of overripeness
a day like a thousand years
    pondering possibilities, walking a few steps ahead,
    cyclical, a sense of direction, leaving
        poor old Klodka[13] behind us:
            And when he rose from the deep
            he was grown old and frail[14]

Stared long into the river
    until eyes moved with the water
westward
    in the dark (blackness being
the beginning of all)
reluctant to turn back
    waterfowl on the wing
        following the barges
caught up in the trellis of midday sunlight
    in the shimmering green of the Oder
        which gathered up the light of the towns
burying it deep down
    to suffuse the fish with it
        on reaching the ocean
that which flashes, drowns, expires: all is part of the process.
Of the millennium: *two lusty journeymen wend their way*[15] ·
    many a barge capsized and sank
        from having shipped too much coal

and too much of the despair
        of those who load the coal

Then in winter the frost of stars
      straight from Siberia
           as foretold by Kotik
and the river ground its teeth
      rose in March
          as spring came
in its white confirmation dress
      causing the bridges to tremble
shattering our vitreous laughter
      into jagged fragments
          between bobbing
ice floes
      shouting at old Klodka our mild imprecations

Our boyhood drowned
      in high water
         a little more each year:
first Antek Bielschowski in the spring of '37
      Karel Jontza and Hottek Sczelski the following year
then, in February '40, Josel Kryczyczek, the Green Angel,
      having been turned that color by waste water
        from the V.O.S. nitrogen plant
his father, a Block Warden, used to sing
      Deutsch ist die Saar
and changed his name to "Kreis"
yet had them chisel
      "Josel Kryczyczek"[16]
        on the headstone

Wednesdays: Ohle   Lohe   Katzbach   Bober & Queis
Lausitzer Neisse:[17] *his craft lay at the bottom*
                and all around was calm
                a cold wind skimmed the water[18]
Went down to the river
      arms stemming against the wind
         closing invisible doors

our laughter blown to shreds
    in the reeds
cutting the river
the green trellis
moves lower
the leaves that cover me
    have a bitter taste:
I hear the thousand voices from the deep[19]

III   THE ROAD TO THE MINE

Still in my ears the engines, the signals
    the bridge a drowsy animal
        that did not budge
freight cars, tracks, electric masts
and the boilers keening
allotments next to the signal cabin
the RAW—"Germany's third largest refitting plant"
there
    somewhere in the confusion of beginnings
this road came into being
    the old amber trade route
scented first by Attila's dogs
trodden hard by countless herds of cattle
traveled over by rickety carts
    with excitedly jabbering Jews
laid out with slag now
    from the Upper Silesian Iron & Steel Mills
topped with stones from Ratibor
    and the resignation of silicotic miners

That was the way to school
the streetcar ran to Königshütte
moj boże kochana:[20] i.e. before
    they put up TALK GERMAN signs
rowan trees in morning haze
    glowing at evening with story-book fire
tanks rattling past
    with dead eyes

the road remained silent
    encompassed by leering lamps
painted over black to leave
    narrow slits of light
the Reich was observing blackout
    the road remained silent
scrawled across the front of the camions: SIEG[21]
    they never asked me where the road led
Cracow, Warsaw or Chenstochowa
    (their maps were all wrong)
I knew it led
    straight to the next world
this came to me at night
    looking out of the window

Molloy pedaled past by day
    on a pushbike
his right leg stiff
    or was it his left?
was it the real Molloy
    or just old Gran'pa Piechotta?
no matter
we went to school
satchels reeking of draff
    like the blackboard wiper
    and our hair and mouth
past the brewers
    with its heady smell
old women carrying cans of light beer
miners queueing for their coal allowance
the beer was as black
    as the coal
        and the tunics of the miners' band
widows in mourning
      the coal which is our livelihood
      killeth us into the bargain
Thus the prayer of old Piechotta

Soldiers
    moving along the road
        straight out of the myth
of the Third Reich
they had trouble learning our lingo
sang songs of the Westerwald
and spelled out *Perunnja*[22]
laid girls in the woods
nothing remains but blackness
widows now, old and forlorn

Still in my ear the engines, the signals
    the bridge a drowsy animal
that did not budge
an outcry from the Hultschinsky Settlement
a fracas with knives
    psalms
the procession to Calvary[23]
words numb with frost
        —Thou who wert betrayed by Thy disciple
        —Thou who wert scourged and tortured
        —Thou who wert nailed to the Cross

All roads lead back to boyhood
but the road to the mine
    of this I am sure
leads up to heaven
    When doomsday comes
        I shall tread you once again

IV

Each new day lops an hour off boyhood
I move my chair nearer the desk
draw on a cigarette
scenes flicker across the retina
    and fade
To fix them in my mind
    I jot down notes:

freight yard . . . steam . . .
engines . . . the turbid
turgid river . . .
the thousand voices from the deep
road to time . . .
highway to Przeskläbje . . .
everlasting boyhood
with images emerging from smoke and dreams and the flames

NOTES

[1] Pistulka: a legendary Robin Hood of the Gleiwitz region.

[2] The broadcast was interrupted by shots at around eight P.M. on August 31, 1939, when a simulated Polish attack was made on the Gleiwitz radio station by a group of six SS men dressed in Polish uniforms and carrying Polish weapons supplied by Admiral Canaris, head of German Intelligence. This was one of several similarly staged incidents used as a pretext for the invasion of Poland one day later.

[3] A line from a German song popular in the 1940s, here sung with a German Silesian accent.

[4] German Silesian accent.

[5] pullock: Polish slang for penis.

[6] dupa: Polish slang for backside, often used in the sense of "idiot."

[7] During the Soviet winter offensive, the survivors of Auschwitz (Oświecim) concentration camp, referred to as "stripies" on account of their camp uniform, were marched in columns into the interior of Germany. One such column passed through Gleiwitz in January 16, 1945.

[8] As Soviet armies continued to advance, hundreds of thousands of German Silesians began fleeing on foot into the interior of Germany.

[9] Przeskläbje: a small, sparsely populated area with numerous gravel and sand pits, situated near Gleiwitz, renamed Laban by the Germans during the war.

[10] Quotation from "The Two Journeymen," by the Upper Silesian poet Joseph von Eichendorff (1788–1857).

[11] Totschka and Huss: Toschka, a Czech Silesian nobleman, and Jan Huss, the Czech religious reformer, were burned as heretics in 1415 by Pope John XXIII.

[12] Oppa, Zinna, Hotzenplotz, Glatzer Neisse: German names of tributaries of the river Odra (Oder).

[13] Klodka: Polish term of endearment for the river Kłodzka (German: Klodnitz), used by Polish and German Silesians alike.

[14-15] From "The Two Journeymen."

[16] Kryczyczek: Polish for "little cross." Kreis: German for "circle." German Silesians with Polish names were forcibly encouraged during the war to assume German names.

[17] Ohle, Lohe, Katzbach, Bober & Queis, Lausitzer Neisse: German names of tributaries of the Odra.

[18-19] From "The Two Journeymen."

[20] *moj boże kochana*: Polish for "Dear God!"

[21] Seig: German for victory.

[22] *Perunnja*: a mild Polish Silesian imprecation also widely used by German Silesians. Perun is the old Slavic god of thunder.

[23] A reference to Góra Swientej Anny (German: Annaberg), a place of pilgrimage.

THE MUSEUM

ROBERT DUNCAN

Grand Architecture that the Muses command! my heart and breathing lungs mount the ascending tones in which your pillars swell, sound, and soar, above the struggling mind. In the treasure room enclosed in sound, Muse upon Muse turns to gaze into the radiant space in building.

In certain designs they are most present, and in their presence I come, I realize, into their design. What I see now is a shadowd space, a shell in time, a silent alcove in thunder, in which the stony everlasting gaze loses itself in my coming into its plan. It is an horizon coming in from what we cannot see to sound in sight that is female. Moving toward an orizon of the visible. From this carving out in thought of an arrival, the figure of a womanly grace invades the sound of the heart that beats for her, and, in number, repeats in a run of alcoves—shadowd radiance upon shadowd radiance—beyond the body of this Woman, the body of these women. In the Museum—as in the labyrinth at Knossos, the Minotaur; as in the head of the Great God, the hawk Horus returning—a Woman that is a Company of Women moves.

She will not devour the heart but holds it high in her command. That shadow she stands in is the shadowing of the heart's ease. Yet now in an exaltation of this chamber my mind comes upon the Bestial Muse, the devouring *Impératrice* at the heart of the Museum. In the inner chambers of the heart of the building, the fountains of blood are all there is. And the laboring pumps that she hides there. And the locks and releases hidden there.

I am entirely hers in that confessional. Entirely shadowd. Entirely gazing. A route of seeing carved in stone. A stream of utter weeping in that stone suspended. And if I were a woman out of the man I am, a Poetess would burst into her lament and memorial for the man destroyed in her.

O Muses, ancient and overwhelming sisters we have so long playd
      in whose
orders, you stand between us and our Father;
you lead us on into this vale between slopes flowery and sweet
      where all
our grievances and memories of love run into song;
you come to meet us at the well you command in the midst of
      our thirst;
you hold us in the suspension of your regard;
and the smile of an appreciation we cannot fathom breaks away
      under us.

In the halls of the Museum all that we meant to remember—our passionate resolve, our crying out and our murmurous sigh—falls into that fame that silences what we were. Was it fame then that we cried out for? Was it fame that we protested? O Muses, aweful and brilliant in your drawing us toward that grace in which the spine is curved into life to sound the depths of its death in fame, your fame catches my tears in its resounding cistern. And every mammal weeping I hear, drip upon drip, as if alone, resounding there. And birds and reptiles weeping. Cell upon cell, in each, this shadow; in each, this Muse of a Commanding Art; in each, this falling into time, drop by drop; in each, this eternal gaze; in each, this ultimate Woman; in each, this guile without guile—the artful suggestion glancing; the terrible amusement; the call to grace that is drawn to dance upon Hurt once more.

Now, deep, deep down in the underground of restraint, the bass intoning of a Man begins, wonderous in its progression Male, its thunderous resolve of a commanding sorrow. It is the Man that men and women have dreamt deep in themselves to be their species —for I came from the body of Woman into the thought of Man— and, all of darkness, that Man in the light of Being groans and turns upon Himself. A challenging tone that begins and passes into the arrest of challenge. O mighty Worm that in the Cocoon of

What Is slumbers! As you turn and intone your turning, the Great
Women in the Hall of the Muses appear to be statues groaning. The
poets whimper in their sheltering shadows, and, from their altars,
poetesses advance to sing once more as Sappho sang from the lyric
strain that Love that breaks us from what we are

irresistible force,
bitter, sweet, that even now strikes us down, you have awakend
what we feard we were, and, men and women, we are lost in you.

Pain
enters Being
drop
by drop

The Earth in its deep foundations shakes
and tears the bindings of ancient structures loose.

The Muses appear to be now
deserted cisterns in a row.

Was there in the beginning
    some vow I made
that has come due? I know
    no more of Art than this—

a kind of play that when I was a child
was fearful in its promise and yet
led from fear into a radiance, a brother's
turning for a sister's kiss.

The Muses fade into dim images.
The images fade as if I made them up
and came out of making into a loss of confidence.

And now . . . *Now . . Now . . Now . .*
the poem sounds its refrain in time:

There cometh now as if it were an ancient return to rime,
behind and beneath the man I am, the sounding of another Man
      I am. Man
in me. Alone. His ultimate aloneness
invading me. Invading my own utter aloneness in my time.
His promise, the promise of what Man *is in me,*
      reaches up and takes
into itself as a persisting need
      that dimness of the other side.

And Him *the gathering of shadowy Muses shakes.*

It is the architecture then of arts inspired by confidences of an earthquake yet to come. The Muses are of stone to be riven from stone. And they gaze—it is the vision of this very art in which out of no confidence their confidential song comes into me—into the abyss they gaze into which the Museum falls.

THE CRAWLERS

RUSSELL EDSON

Personae: Father, heavy set, middle-aged, bald man, wearing a dark suit; a businessman. Daughter, a fat woman in her forties, wearing a shapeless housecoat, her hair set in little pin curls. Man (Daughter's suitor), in his thirties, thin; wears a cheap suit with a tasteless tie.

Father and daughter are sitting in a living room. Father is looking at his daughter. She seems unaware, as if simply another piece of furniture.

FATHER. If you were two daughters you would still be two horribly fat women.

DAUGHTER. (*Without animation*) Goo goo, da da . . .

FATHER. Stop that hideous baby talk! You are not at all cute. You must try to hide your gluttony with a quiet dignity.

DAUGHTER. (*Exaggerated haughtiness*) Like this, Daddy dear?

FATHER. . . . A kind of wistful reserve; for any exaggerated behavior only points to your exaggerated bulk. I've invited a young man from the office to meet you tonight . . .

DAUGHTER. Oh, daddy!

FATHER. Even for all your gluttony, my daughter, disadvantage that it is, you are blessed with a rich father. Young men are prisoners in their desire to be rich. They are in particular awe of my office chair, with all its squeaks and grunts, the torn leather, the splintering wood; which, in symbol, one must admit, is like a throne . . .

DAUGHTER. Oh daddy, you bore me with your silly old chair. I want to talk about romance, and all you want to talk about is your dumb old business.

FATHER. You better be glad I have a dumb old business, so I can buy you a husband—yes, I'm buying you a husband. I'm making an utter stranger an heir, just so you'll have reason to go to bed at night, instead of sitting around all night making baby sounds, as I try to read my newspaper . . .

DAUGHTER. Is he pretty?

FATHER. How do I know, am I a homosexual? I don't look at men that way. One might say he looks healthy.

DAUGHTER. Is he awful nice, daddy?

FATHER. He's one of those shoe kissers. A terrible habit. One cannot tell how far up the leg it might go. Yet, who wouldn't come to my feet, gladly? Am I not almost a king, is my business not almost an empire? . . . Ah, but there is something so secondhand about him, a used floor model; damaged merchandise that should be sent back to the factory; in this case, back to his mother, either for re-use of the parts, or total repair . . . But this is no longer a buyer's market . . . My God, I don't envy the poor man . . .

DAUGHTER. Do you think he'll come to my feet?

FATHER. I said he was a shoe kisser. Shoe kissers usually have a good nose for wealth. He'll probably begin the evening at my shoes. Then, when I tell him all that is mine will be yours, he'll likely find your shoes just as kissable. I do wish you wouldn't wear those sneakers, they smell.

DAUGHTER. Oh, I wish he would just kiss me directly on my epidermis.

FATHER. Epidermis?—where did you ever learn such a terrible word?

DAUGHTER. Maybe I should sit upside down on my chair, with my feet in the air, and my face hanging down on the floor; then he'll kiss my lips.

FATHER. I suppose with your epidermis showing; so that he'll not only think you fat, but bearded . . . Oh my dear, just be patient, if everything works out properly, there'll not be a place on you he'll not kiss. But don't frighten him away with odd postures. Your heft only points to itself when you start acting oddly.

DAUGHTER. Da da, goo goo . . .

FATHER. Are you starting that baby talk again?

DAUGHTER. I really think I ought to talk baby talk, it makes me seem cute.

FATHER. You are anything but cute.

DAUGHTER. (*Blinking eyes and taking other, so-called, cute poses*) Da da da da . . .

FATHER. Goddamn you, Goddamn you . . .

DAUGHTER. Goo goo (*Hiccup*) da da (*Hiccup*).

FATHER. . . . Dirty slob . . . Dirty fat slob . . .

DAUGHTER. Maybe I should put on a baby bonnet, and a lace bib? . . .

FATHER. You're an aging fat woman. Why do you want to pretend to be an infant? You look like a drooling imbecile . . .

DAUGHTER. Daddy, look at this. (*Tongue hanging from her mouth, eyes blinking, limbs jerking with the useless motions of an infant*) Da da, goo goo.

FATHER. No no no! It's hideous! Why do you refuse to be dignified?

DAUGHTER. Look at this, daddy, (*Wags head, crosses eyes, and waves hands*)

FATHER. If you continue I'll punch you in the face. I'll kick you in your stomach, you bitch; you dirty fat bitch!

DAUGHTER. (*Starts to cry*) Why do you want to hurt me; just when I'm trying to make myself attractive? You don't know how lonely I've been. Men like baby dolls who wear diapers.

FATHER. Yes, cute young women with pert young bodies, wearing brassieres . . .

DAUGHTER. (*Supports breasts in hands, pulls them up*) What's wrong with these?

FATHER. Don't do that . . .

DAUGHTER. (*Rubs hefty thighs*) —Plenty of everything.

FATHER. Too much of everything.

DAUGHTER. Da da . . . Maybe I should wear a diaper? . . .

FATHER. I'm warning you, you're going to get a punch right in the stomach.

DAUGHTER. (*Tough voice*) Are you kidding? I could break you in half.

FATHER. (*Lunges*) Okay, you asked for it. (*He punches her in her stomach.*)

DAUGHTER. You dirty son of a bitch . . .

FATHER. (*Punches daughter on jaw*) Wow, that feels good! (*Daughter falls to floor and is still.*)

(*A few seconds pass, father is panting after set-to with daughter; pause, and then a scratching and mild tapping at the door; father answers the door, it is the young man.*)

FATHER. Come in, my boy.

(*Awkward thin man comes in, looking nervously over shoulder as if expecting to be followed; blinks with hands moving oddly.*)

FATHER. Sit down, sit down. Here, let me get you a drink.

(*The man opens his mouth wide at father, as if he were adjusting his face.*)

FATHER. (*Ignores strange behavior; pours drink*) I'd like you to meet my daughter. (*Gestures toward unconscious daughter on floor*)

(*Young man sits on couch with hands folded, eyes move foolishly about.*)

FATHER. Now, sir, no use beating about the bush; my daughter will be a very rich woman someday—and . . . well . . . you have eyes; it would be foolish of me to attempt to hide the fact that she is most unattractive, fortyish, and overweight . . .

MAN. Yippee, I'm gonna be rich, I'm gonna be rich!

FATHER. You might pretend to feel something for my daughter.

MAN. What . . . ? Who . . . ?

FATHER. . . . . That you have some of the manly feelings for a woman.

MAN. I'm going to be rich, then I shall not have to deal with scum like you.

FATHER. Who do you think you're talking to?

MAN. Oh, I heard that someplace.

FATHER. I see . . . However, there are certain arrangements to be made, marriage certificate, leg hobbles . . . But don't misunderstand me, the leg hobbles are not punitive; just a precaution against your running away . . .

MAN. Running away?

FATHER. Well, you have merely to look at my daughter to understand the precaution.

MAN. But leg hobbles . . . How about the coitus—or is that not part of it?

FATHER. Aren't we getting a little ahead of ourselves?

MAN. Does she always do it on the floor?

FATHER. My daughter is merely being unconscious; you mustn't think she's trying to tempt you. Unfortunately I was forced to take a little disciplinary action, and she blacked out.

(*Man sticks tongue out and wags it, rolls eyes and shakes head.*)

FATHER. Why do you act like that?

MAN. Like what? (*Repeats action.*)

FATHER. Like that.

MAN. Oh, if you don't like me, I'll leave.

FATHER. No no, now don't get like that; don't be so sensitive.

MAN. Maybe you want me to kiss your shoes. I will if you want . . .

FATHER. Please don't start that.

MAN. No no, really, I'm quite willing. I'll get right down on my hands and knees, and crawl over to your feet. Really, it would be my pleasure . . .

FATHER. I said, no; I do not require that.

MAN. Come on, I'm perfectly willing. (*Gets down on hands and knees*) Look, see, I'm on my hands and knees.

FATHER. Get the hell back on the couch. You act like a pervert.

MAN. Why, just because I'm humble . . . Maybe you're working me up to something even more humiliating. I'm willing, you name it.

FATHER. I want you to marry my daughter; I'll make a rich man of you . . .

MAN. Okay, let's get it over with, drop your pants.

FATHER. What are you suggesting!

MAN. I'm willing to do it; but I'm not going to talk about it.

FATHER. Would you like a punch in the face?

MAN. Do I have to?

FATHER. I asked you here tonight for my daughter.

MAN. You mean you don't want me? (*Starts to cry*)

FATHER. It isn't that; you're a lovely person, I'm sure; and if I were *that* way, why . . .

MAN. You're just saying that.

FATHER. No, I mean it. You could be quite attractive . . . Why, if only you were a woman, why, I . . . Don't cry; after all, there are so many wonderful things in the world, ice-cream sodas, rides on the carrousel . . .

MAN. No no, you don't like me.

FATHER. I like you very much. But, you see, I'm not *that* way.

MAN. Oh yes you are; that's why it hurts . . .

FATHER. I am not! Even when I was a little boy my father used to say I was every inch a man. If anything, I have always been overly masculine. Father even gave me a rifle to shoot when I was yet only a child.

MAN. But you look like my mother.

FATHER. Well, a man has a right to relax. Being a man is hard work. I've spent my life being overly masculine. Don't you think I have a right to be a woman at my age? I've earned it.

MAN. I want to be a woman, too.

FATHER. Well, you've got to earn it.

MAN. If I marry your daughter, then can I be a woman?

FATHER. Oh the devil take your conditions; any other man would jump at the chance to be rich.

MAN. I would do anything to be rich.

FATHER. You understand, then, that the marriage is binding; leg hobbles and all . . .

MAN. You can't expect me to crawl with leg hobbles; perhaps you will crawl to me? . . .

FATHER. I do not crawl to any man. Perhaps my daughter will crawl to you.

MAN. Yes, we shall crawl together, like sisters, rivals for your affection, daddy dear.

FATHER. I'm not taking you in as a daughter. I'm buying my own real daughter a husband.

MAN. Oh will you buy me one, too?

FATHER. I don't owe you anything. Why should I buy you a husband?

MAN. If you expect me to be your daughter . . .

FATHER. But, I don't want you to be my daughter.

MAN. You don't like me. (*Starts to cry*)

FATHER. Oh don't start that again. Please, you're a very nice man.

MAN. No. you don't like me . . .

FATHER. I think you're very nice . . .

MAN. Should I kiss your shoes? (*Gets on hands and knees*)

FATHER. No no, don't do that!

MAN. You're making a fool of me; you're cruel.

FATHER. Please, don't feel bad . . . When my daughter comes awake there will be no end of the things she'll let you do.

MAN. You brought me up here to ridicule me.

FATHER. No, don't say that. (*Pets man's head*)

(*With exaggerated affection, man starts to kiss father's hand.*)

FATHER. (*Withdraws hand with disgust*) Don't do that!

MAN. (*Begins to cry again*) You don't like me.

FATHER. Well, the truth is, I don't. I just simply cannot like you.

MAN. You just brought me up here to ridicule me.

FATHER. I brought you up here—you came up here yourself, sir . . . I admit at my invitation, but for my daughter, only . . . You mustn't think . . . Why, that's quite out of the question . . .

MAN. (*Still on hands and knees*) Now shall I kiss your shoes?

FATHER. I'm getting rather sick of this. Are you going to marry my daughter or not?

MAN. That's how we arranged it, isn't it?

FATHER. Arranged what?

MAN. I could have been your secretary . . .

FATHER. I don't need a secretary.

MAN. And that's why I have to marry your daughter.

FATHER. That's not why; that has nothing to do with it.

MAN. Didn't you arrange it this way so I could be near you?

FATHER. What are you thinking?

MAN. (*Crying again*) You don't like me. At the office, under those flattering fluorescent lights, you thought you liked me. But now, after seeing me in your home, you've decided against having me with you.

FATHER. Please, don't cry . . . I think you're a lovely chap. (*Looks at audience, shrugs, and looks as if having tasted something putrid*) But it's my daughter who needs you.

MAN. You're not fooling me, that's your mother on the floor, pretending to be unconscious—anyway, your father would never give his wife's hand in marriage.

FATHER. My father has nothing to do with this. Besides, that's his granddaughter.

MAN. Wait a minute, this is a trap. You're a female cop disguised as that woman's grandfather.

FATHER. No, honestly, I'm the father . . . What's all this? . . . Surely, I don't look like a grandfather?

MAN. Sometimes it's a trick; you get invited someplace, and it turns out to be a trap; a policeman will pretend to be a man.

FATHER. Well, they are men. What are you talking about?

MAN. You're sure you're not a policewoman disguised as a businessman selling his daughter?

FATHER. Why are you so suspicious?

MAN. I've had trouble before.

FATHER. What trouble?

MAN. Never mind. That's why I carry a gun.

FATHER. A gun? You're frightening me.

MAN. Scared, huh?

FATHER. I'm not afraid of you.

MAN. Please don't be afraid.

FATHER. I'm not afraid. Why should I be afraid?

MAN. No, really, I won't hurt you.

FATHER. I said I'm not afraid of you.

MAN. Admit it.

FATHER. Admit what?

MAN. You're afraid; it's natural.

DAUGHTER. (*Begins to come awake*) Da da, goo goo . . .

FATHER. (*To man*) Do you want what she got?

MAN. What?

FATHER. —Right in the stomach, and a left to the jaw!

MAN. You wouldn't hit me?

DAUGHTER. Da da (*Hiccup*), da da (*Hiccup*).

MAN. I'll kiss your shoes.

DAUGHTER. (*Hiccup hiccup hiccup*) Goo.

MAN. (*Aware of daughter's baby sounds*) What's that?

FATHER. Oh, I'm sorry—this is my daughter. (*To daughter*) And this is your future husband . . .

DAUGHTER. Daddy, where are you? (*Reaches feebly out like an infant*)

FATHER. (*To man*) Help your darling up.

MAN. (*Looks at daughter*) Is it mother?

FATHER. Mother of the Species, heh heh . . .

DAUGHTER. (*Starts acting in her usual cute manner, hiccupping and burping*) Da da, goo goo . . .

MAN. It's mama; mama mama mama . . . (*Runs to daughter, embracing and kissing her*)

FATHER. (*To audience*) It's disgusting.

DAUGHTER. Goo goo, da da, &c.

MAN. You're not mother. It's a trap!

DAUGHTER. What's the difference, soldier boy?

MAN. No no, you are not my mother.

DAUGHTER. (*Exaggerated sex stance*) Come on, sailor boy.

FATHER. (*To daughter*) Easy, easy; get the hook in his mouth.

DAUGHTER. Why don't you come up and see me sometime?

FATHER. Easy, easy; let out some line . . .

MAN. (*With sudden change of pace; with commanding voice*) Okay, this is an arrest. (*Pulls badge out*)

FATHER. You're a cop!

MAN. That's right, attached to the morals division. I'm going to have to run you in for suggestive obscenity.

FATHER. Your Honor, I've done nothing; I plead innocent.

MAN. You've been suggesting all evening that I kiss your shoes.

FATHER. I asked you up here for my daughter.

MAN. Same thing, white slavery.

FATHER. But but but but but . . .

MAN. It's too late.

FATHER. No, wait, listen, I'll kiss your shoes if you'll forget what you've seen.

MAN. Trying to bribe an officer; compounding the charges.

FATHER. All right, all right, I'll go down on my hands and knees . . .

MAN. You're only making it worse for yourself.

FATHER. (*On hands and knees*) Look, I'll crawl over to your feet. Really, it would be my pleasure . . .

MAN. Can't you understand that the game is over; that you're trapped?

FATHER. Come on, I'm perfectly willing. I'm on my hands and knees . . .

DAUGHTER. Daddy!

FATHER. Not now, dear. (*To man*) . . . Working me up to something more humiliating? I'm willing, you name it.

DAUGHTER. Daddy, he's mine!

FATHER. Not now, dear; can't you see I'm trying to avoid prison?

DAUGHTER. But he's mine.

FATHER. I'm fighting for my life, and all you can think of is sex.

DAUGHTER. I want sex.

FATHER. I'll buy you all kinds of men. But now I'm fighting to clear my good name with the law. (*To man*) Sir, please . . .

MAN. Look at my badge. (*Hands badge to father*) Would you have me disgrace it?

FATHER. (*Reads aloud from badge*) *Junior G-Man* . . . An important man down on his hands and knees, begging to be humiliated. I can't believe that a man of my importance is to be found on his hands and knees in front of his daughter's suitor, asking, begging . . .

MAN. We all crawl one time or another, don't we, sir?

FATHER. You are quite right. I had forgotten how to crawl. Thank you for showing me again. I remember how I crawled up in the business world. I had quite a figure some years ago, and it didn't go unnoticed. I made important men sitting behind enormous desks crawl across the floor to me. I polished my shoes carefully with hypnotic luster wax . . .

DAUGHTER. I want to crawl across the floor to him. (*On hands and knees*) Really, it would be my pleasure . . .

FATHER. People must crawl to me. Anyone has sexual desire, but who has the money to afford it? I could crawl, I proved that a few moments ago. But who knows which of us will not yet turn out to be a policeman . . .

DAUGHTER. But, daddy, you said you were buying me a husband.

FATHER. Of course. But all this crawling business tends to ignite a certain crawling desire that begins at the feet—we are all crawlers at heart!

MAN. Don't let her crawl toward me.

FATHER. Things always look worse than they are. The thing is to face them. The imagination is far more fearful than reality.

MAN. No no, I would crawl toward something. One has control that way. One can always stop and go the other way.

FATHER. Yes yes, we like to crawl toward things. That's how we keep things from crawling toward us. You are so right!

DAUGHTER. Daddy, may I crawl to you?

FATHER. Oh no, dear child, for as attractive as . . .

DAUGHTER. Really, it would be my pleasure . . .

FATHER. Oh no, dear child, for as attractive as . . .

DAUGHTER. I'm humble; maybe you're working me up to something more humiliating?

FATHER. Oh no, dear child, for as attractive as . . .

DAUGHTER. Okay, okay . . . I'm willing; let's get it over with, drop your pants.

FATHER. Oh no, dear child . . . for as attractive as your offer may seem, still, the biology of our relationship, and the differences in our ages, not to mention the illegality, or the fact that you are most unattractive, being in your forties and quite overweight . . . And the late hour, and a number of other things that work against such a consummation . . . Besides which, I'm your father . . .

DAUGHTER. *Father?* But you said you were going to marry me.

FATHER. (*Pointing to man*) He's going to marry you.

DAUGHTER. Then why are you trying to humiliate me, making me get down on my hands and knees and crawling to you?

FATHER. No such a thing, I was trying to keep you off.

DAUGHTER. Why do you want to hurt me, just when I'm trying to be attractive? You don't know how lonely I've been. Men like women to crawl to them.

FATHER. But I'm a married man. Don't you remember, I married your mother some years ago.

DAUGHTER. Da da (*Hiccup*) goo goo, da da . . .

FATHER. No no, not that way.

DAUGHTER. Then what way? You don't want me to crawl, and you don't want me to be cute . . .

MAN. Is it my turn?

FATHER. For what?

MAN. To crawl.

FATHER. To whom?

MAN. One just crawls, because there is no other way.

FATHER. Why does everyone have to crawl? There are other ways; there are ice-cream sodas and rides on the carrousel . . .

DAUGHTER. It makes the woman's arse so much more attractive as it grinds along humiliated in the dust of human approval. Besides, it's nice to be close to the ground in case there's some change lying around.

FATHER. But, you're a rich woman, you don't need change.

DAUGHTER. Everyone needs a change, do you think I want to go on like this the rest of my life?

MAN. And what of me, I'm not a rich woman?

FATHER. You're not a woman.

MAN. That doesn't mean I couldn't do with some change . . .

FATHER. Yes, that makes sense, we could all do with a change.

(*All get on hands and knees, and crawl off stage.*)

ELEVEN POEMS

CID CORMAN

1
The rain re-
lentlessly
effortless

It makes us
look like fools
trying so

hard to be
what we are—·
which we are.

2
Me
assure
you?

How—
if a
breath—

your
breath—does
not?

3
I'm thinking
of
saying . . .

Say it.
Isn't now
al-

ready
a
memory?

4
To embrace
a tree—how
silly can
you get—yet

To want to
dance with it
the way the
wind's doing.

5
Sun in
the window—
an eye

for an
eye awa-
kening.

6
Down the street
someone else
dead. Unknown

but close. How
near next is
distances.

7
Night arrives.
It is not
far to be

going. It
is not far
to have gone.

8
Even the monkey
reaching down for the
moon in the river

with his other hand
clings to the bare branch
without thinking why.

9
Is there any
sense to being
that saying so

does not deny
and equally
at loss confirm?

10
No way
to say

enough
enough.

11
What is life
a man asks

Only a
man replies.

A CITY

ANDREW GLAZE

Running from the pestilence,
bringing it with me,
ringing in a waist-high Henry J like a peal of bells,
I flapped, with daughter, dog and friend,
whistling North from the South
like a feckless peanut steamer,
a fierce and impossible freight
bounded before and behind
like an automatic piano waltz,
staggering around and far away
the Amboys and Bayonne,
(the bridge like a ring with a diamond,
rusting off right,
with the road bent to Red Hook).
Who was the gift giver, and pledged
what fortune for this prize?
Oh flats and steeples of Jersey City!
A country trembled immaculately like
a holy dream in the red-hanging hall
accursed in the eyes of a drunk.
Clapping aside the nacreous veils of luckless magic,
we passed into sight of the tall sails
of the hundred masted city!
Shining like glass in the blazing lens of the sun.

This was my winnings, my castle, my island!
For all the never-at-home in the world
is there not a city?
I slipped through its door like a thief.

.   .   .

They were sitting in the grass,
and needed a wash.
But down on dirty knees
they stretched out the shivering taffeta,
the silver plastic on bamboo,
and then, let it go.
Away——away——up like smoke
shaken and dazed like a big fierce bat-wing,
it bucked and rode
through the cold teething of the air,
it flew against a thunderhead
over dark New Jersey,
touching the infinite verges of blue waste.
There, like a wavering neat star,
it hung and blew,
until with a sudden wink,
it snapped in the hazy fetterings of space,
and the star twitched and dissolved,
flicked out like an eye.
One of them got to his feet,
his gold teeth gleaming,
his fingers making knots,
his face stared hungrily
up at its empty square.
The wind boxed the collar about his ears.
He stretched and shuddered.
His friend dropped a pebble on his foot.
He cursed. At the roofless sky
he aimed a witless cuff.
They knelt and began to flatten out another.

.   .   .

Didn't I always want to be the man
walking in the rain,
coming down the dark street?
Didn't I want to be the rain?
Simmering in front of the bus barn,
slashing under car wheels like confetti,
and the lightning,
shearing aluminum foil
in giant notches
across the crumpling sky?
And the lights blooming in soft puddles,
and the wet policeman
flapped over by the swinging awning?
Didn't I want to be myself,
naked in the window,
and the stinging of the thousand
flying water needles?
All of them—

. . .

My daughter, just at the age of eleven,
busy coming down from the bus, looked up,
like a pop queen,
and all of a sudden the omens turned bad,
the eggs gave in on their shells.
Her straw hat
was bent forward caplike
to show me its raddled pony in red and blue
galloping across the straw-colored field
of the crown.
A porter pushed her happiness
ahead of him on the cart.
My heart made an audible knock.
What chatelaine of the world was this?
And whose prerogative was it
gave such a mistress of manors permission?
That she should bring it home to me,
and give it back like a game,

for what report could I make to her
of all those countries and persons
accounted mothers and fathers, designed to be trusted,
and she was invested in,
that had failed?
How could I throw it far from her in the grass
like a dog to run for my humble news like a bone?

       •   •   •

And of course there came fire sermons
paying for the assassinations of that year,
red, rising like flak
from the zone of the burnt cloud.
Silver cigars like dirigibles slithered.
Cables flamed with messages from God.
Ultimatums rocketed up like light ladders,
brimming over and swimming down.
The wires of the rain fell, stretched out.
Telephone boxes and dead taxis
overflowed with burning zealous calls.
All mine, the whirling spatterdash of howling visual kisses!
Was it gone or to come, or was it only rumor,
the one warm moon
in the velvet waste without eyes,
the bottomless thicket
guarding the lost root?

       •   •   •

Something was being divided up.
The last tags of the unfinished artist's life,
hung from the truck like rags. The painter friend,
with stupendous études set out under the moon
of ten-foot-high burnt-sienna banners,
and six thousand blue-green chickens glued to the Bay Bridge,
trailed from the footboard.
That part had left us which was neat, tight, sensible,
deserted us and gone to midtown.
What was left was divided, loaded, and hanging,

dangled off or fell behind in the street
from the twisted body of the bent Mack,
drinking beer with the driver,
falling underneath in the cobbles with the drunks.
And my shirttail now was falling out
like viscous spittle blowing
or the dirty clothes of luck.

.   .   .

This country of the sidewalk, consider it,
with its all-night-long songs of passion and candles,
and a hunger whose name is murder the trees,
beating out songs of tenderness about them,
hungry to piss on them,
loud like the streetlife of Corinth or Thebes.
Kicking out cans of beer
from the crack of the door,
clinging like flies in the blood of the day,
they played the torero side-slashed by the bull,
or stretched out trash can tops like shields,
pulled thin gloriously
for one perfect gladiatorial moment,
waiting for the acclamations of the president
of the afternoon, all night.
Around them, bright as a victory plate,
cop cars forming in shining rings,
pressing their weight for the ritual stamp
to that thing worth doing
which proffers its gift for a price.

.   .   .

Ai! Ai! for I am the Waltz of the Garbage,
whose battallions of sign bearers
beat their plaques into butterfly wings,
into zig-zags between cars.
There are shattered breakers of glass
like combers over the shores of my curbs.
The lights of fistulas hum in my cabs.

Faces of angry clowns toss grimacings
in smoking handfuls up through the windows
of clubs like bombs.
I discover the name of my city,
I christen it Mont Pelée,
I duck head down in the mail-run of lava.
I toss my hot pennies,
that sing to me of peace on the way.
Peace, that sounds like squadrons of wings of flies.
Insults change like suits of my clothes,
they shy up at the moon
and ricochet back from my foul-mouthed mothers.
That old woman who blows past
sadly looping in the wind, mourns,
as she wavers, "eheu! eheu!
what punishment for me!
What hounds me for all the hundred sins
that a thousand times
I steadfastly hated,
that I would never consider to do."
While down in the subway caves,
see, madmen are sitting,
hiding in electric excavations
calibrating bones.
Scratching graffiti for signs of rain,
they master their horoscopes,
an eternal snow shovels down
whose cigarette papers flutter about like clouds
of the flowing pedestrian feet
that trudge and whirl to the caverns below.
Oh Waltz of the Garbage,
swaying in an air revolving with fires and screams,
your rage, like sunbeams, like music and come-ons,
is riddled like sieves with subliminal wishes of whores!
Oh Waltz of the Garbage,
virulent dance where our lovers are dying,
we push them along through the gutters of going home,
bounce them through boutiques of dirty words
and past vintage years of the dregs of sewage foam,
we bestride them like horses of racing mud-black,

we speed them like mad kings to burial in stores,
we spin our sirens upside down,
backward, we clang our bells.

•   •   •

When the rat climbs up our toilet from the drain,
coming in from the sewer out of the sinking
tenements nearby, shucked of their brick like corn,
he glares at us with the wild incessant eye
that lifts the top of the seat.
Busy, he starts out. Quickly we slam the door,
on the salt, chlorine, ammonia gift
we pitch down to him with a wild clatter,
piling up dead weights on the white tank.
Later, we find him limp, a floating
foot-long, seething kitten, and throw him out
with the trash. He bangs in the can,
but still has become some way, and partly, the winner.
For late at night, after the trucks are gone,
and the stars run green, we hear him thump,
and run and sit on the bland white bowl
of our lives with its eye like the heart of a curse.
And wonder what we have done to make him come
and scuttle about our dregs and skulk with our fear
in the bitter basement draining our slums of thought.

•   •   •

It was twelve years in all,
before what was brought with us and what was provided
and what had been and what would be
became the ends of the same encountering choice.

It was a day of no reasons, that came when the
Hare Krishnas danced past the river, under the sky
like a blue temple bell, in their happy mindless orange
robes of smiles, their barren heads and blue
nose lobes, and they were chanting, westering
down Seventy-second Street, elaborating drums
and bell sounds riverward into the park.

I watched them go, and turning, came upon
Chase and Valda propped like tired dolls
in La Crêpe, with under their elbows crumpled paper
and crumbs of a pancake.
Over their figures, a waitress presided
deeper in shadow, whirling like light in the corner,
and spirals, and turned and came, wearing a grand
baroque blue Breton lace chemise and tall choker
and hat, and some bird croaked like a metal shriek,
re-making somewhere, something else.
Was it the pattern of eaves,
the rounded cornices, buckles, loops and anagrams
of the vast lace in stone of the Hotel Ansonia
across the street? That spirit of Paris
racing in eighteen ninety-five, that totally
unconscious building split with brains and verve,
as Stanford White saw it, drunk one morning on form,
who was going to swallow a bullet walking his garden, soon,
for Evelyn Nesbitt, in the name of Harry K. Thaw
—and these two friends—and my wife,
and the Breton girl, and the Hare Krishnas,
the sun and the finger bells, came dropping
like links of recollection knitting a chain,
and sorted themselves with a foolish ticking sound
about the cornice of some all-circumferential,
proud, confetti and firework devising law. What insane gift
to sense a god-tremendous fearful arch of wands, jets,
circles, creepers of three billion half-mad lives
intersecting, intertwined, that I was tight
anchored to, as well as the hateful enemy-lover of?
Tendrils grew to the ends of my fingers
and into the ground beyond, which was itself,
I could not shake them off, as I was also,
the holy city I looked for but could not find.
All wishes were leading to and from the root,
all things were secretly meeting each other
in assignations at dirty hotels.
Earth would be answered in the end,
however blind the reach and call.

JAMES PURDY'S *I AM ELIJAH THRUSH*

TONY TANNER

Imagine a critic whose preferences and prejudices when it comes to modern American fiction have been formed by a regular reading of, say, Saul Bellow, Norman Mailer, and John Updike—what might he be expected to say about a novel with the following scenario? The narrator is a young black, Albert Peggs, in love with a golden eagle; he becomes involved with an aging actor, "mime, poet, and painter" called Elijah Thrush, who is himself in love with his mute great-grandson. He also becomes the memoirist of an heiress, Millicent de Frayne, who stopped growing old in 1913 when she fell in love with Elijah Thrush. All four of these people, plus the bird, are linked together in a number of ways which takes the book far beyond the simply narrative. Albert's account outlines the frightening (and comic) ascendancy of Millicent over all of them, a series of preemptive power plays which culminates in a funereal wedding banquet on board a ship at sea. Albert is last heard taking over, from the doomed Elijah, Elijah's role in his theater.

Our imaginary critic may well be tempted to dismiss it as perverse farce, a weird homoerotic daydream or nightmare, a frivolous and mannered piece of idiosyncratic surrealism, in all cases lacking the sort of pained "relevance" which he feels he can find among his preferred novelists. This, I fear, is how some American critics are going to receive James Purdy's most recent novel, of which the above scenario is a crude outline. Purdy has never, it seems to me, been done justice by many of the leading contemporary critics, and one reason, it may be, is that they simply don't know how to read his work properly. "Relevance" is an elusive and often impoverishing concept, and it should not be felt that long ruminating monologues on modern times, or the dying embers of naturalism, constitute the most direct or even the most compelling ways of contacting present realities. There is such a thing as indirect relevance as well, and it can offer us riches and subtleties not attainable by headlong assaults on contemporaneity. Since I think it would be an act of injustice to undervalue this hauntingly serious and beautifully written book, I would like to suggest some of the ways in which it touches, in its own unique way, on matters which concern all of us.

We can say straightway that the book centers on various kinds of parasitism, vampirism, sponging, addictions, and habits; the appropriation of some vital part of a person—semen or soul, blood or youth—by a resolute predator. We keep encountering the feeder and the few, host and guest, the devourer and the devoured. Millicent is a very determined feeder, constantly pressing strange foods, rare delicacies, exotic potions and elixirs on Albert, just as she pours her words in his ear and thrusts money onto his poverty. However, forced bounty is no bounty at all, but an act of implacable will, and in seeming to give most Millicent in fact takes all. Albert is the main donor: metaphorically to Millicent and Elijah who in turn bestow on him unexpected rewards and uninvited projections; literally to his golden eagle which he feeds from his living flesh, a "habit" gradually displayed by his feelings for Elijah and Millicent and the great-grandson. Love, here as so often in Purdy's work, tends to be a sickness rather than a satisfaction. His world is full of love, but love which takes distorted forms, failing, or being frustrated, in what might be true attachments. Everywhere there are annihilating failures of recognition, leaving us with a sense of lonely incomplete identities vaporizing back into the void, unfinished because unloving or unloved. Here then is a manifestly serious theme—people living off each other without loving each other—as serious in Purdy as in Hawthorne and James.

But this is only part of the novel. For instance, we gradually notice that the book is full of birds. Albert has his golden eagle, Elijah Thrush (sic) calls his great-grandson "Bird of Heaven," and, though mute, the boy articulates in bird song. Albert is referred to as "black eagle," and so on. This is not purely gratuitous. Some sense of the mystery of birds is as old as history. In Purdy's story "Home by Dark," the grandfather says to the boy: "Birds are really strange creatures. . . . They remember always where to go, where to build their nests, where to return to. . . ." Such a notion of birds would necessarily be attractive to directionless, unhoused, or mishoused modern man. Since Purdy's book is set in New York, where man is not only, like all men, earthbound, but congested, claustrophobic deep in the "behavioral sink," the high incidence of birds moving through the words of the book does seem to hold out the invitation and temptation of a higher, cleaner realm.

This novel suggests more than it says, and keeps its secrets in the midst of revelation. It is a book which devours its own allegories, but not before we have glimpsed their outlines. Thus, for instance, at one level the book is about the fate of America. The Bird of Heaven has "wild Indian eyes" and wears an Indian suit—he is silent, even as the voice of the Indian is no longer heard in the land. Albert is black and comes from Alabama, but like so many displaced blacks he has come North. Elijah was brought up in Illinois and Nebraska but has been drawn East to become a theatrical role-player. Millicent we take to be quintessentially New York. The Indian and the black have their original beauty, but neither of them is at home in the society and the language that surrounds them. More to the point, the aging parts of America need something the black and the Indian have, to keep themselves going. The love is there, but it goes wrong, and no vitalizing, mutually enriching connections are established. The different fragments of America no more compose a unity in the book than they do in real life. And the fact that it is the black narrator who keeps the "almost extinct" golden eagle alive, suggests something about the tenuous continuities of the authentic natural life of America. Millicent kills the eagle, stuffs it, and serves up the meat at the wedding feast. Is this what the whites have done to America?

From the start, Purdy's work has revealed an intense awareness of all that can go grievously and damagingly wrong in the family unity. He has portrayed unparented children, unchilded parents, the unreal father, the mother who possesses or relinquishes at the wrong times. And in the absence of an actual family, he has shown all manner of would-be surrogate parents and guardians, and has explored the adoptive inclination to uncanny depth. In many of his short stories (and Purdy is one of the most accomplished writers in this genre to have appeared in America), we find some disruption or failure of the family. In *I Am Elijah Thrush*, there is no actual legitimized family, but this allows Purdy to explore the notion of the family in broader terms. Can there, indeed, be an American family? From the start Albert, who seems to retain no notion of his real parents, senses some compelling involvement, even identity, with the strange white couple who effectively take him over. Millicent uses Albert ruthlessly and heartlessly, but as he says, "only a mother could have been so cruel," an idea more emphatically echoed at the wedding banquet when she announces to Albert, "I am your mother"; while soon after Elijah addresses Albert as "my child," and Albert himself has "the giddy feeling I was being present at the marriage of my own parents." We may feel that Albert is at last "parented." This prepares us for the climax. Elijah owns a theater at which he dances a variety of roles. As the wedding ship draws him away from America, helpless in Millicent's clutches, he sends out one last message to Albert (this time through a megaphone, as communication is rapidly fading). His instruction is to keep his theater open and "play all my roles." Thus at the end, Albert comes forward on stage and announces with a sob, "I am Elijah Thrush." He isn't, manifestly, but as "son" and "inheritor" he has adopted the imposed identity. What Elijah has had to relinquish, Albert will take on; the young black takes over from the aging white. He could, thereby, be maintaining a threatened continuity, and what is more natural for the son to take the place of the dethroned, if not the defunct father? At the same time, it is an ambiguous declaration, for if he is Elijah Thrush, where has Albert Peggs gone? It could be the final victory for the white people to make him negate his black identity in order to perpetuate their theatricalized mythologies.

Let's take a closer look at the members of the family. Millicent has all the power, though her role is not without its poignancy (Purdy is, incidentally, one of the few American writers who seem to understand women). She has a hand like a claw, a tongue like a cow's, the strength of a man. She seems to grow taller in her imperiousness, and both Albert and Elijah find themselves on the floor in front of her more than once. She gives Elijah his clothes, his cosmetics, and—a possibility conceded by Elijah—perhaps his very existence. Elijah is a true mesmerist, an old man who can nevertheless play the "reincarnation" of the Most Beautiful Man in

the World. In his theater he holds his audience in raptures with his
erotic and hedonistic dances. On the walls there are pictures show-
ing the Mime as "Hiawatha, the child Moses, Apollo, and Jesus in
the Garden with Mary Magdalene"; Indian boy, Hebrew prophet,
Greek God, Christ the redeemer; beauty, wisdom, light, salvation
—or a parodistic salmagundi of these once revered figures. Where
Millicent demands total "concession" and obedience, Elijah asks for
"total fidelity, total oneness." Either way, their attitudes seem to
contain little respect for the independent otherness of people, for in
their different ways they are both engorgers. Their marriage is
scarcely a happy one, though it might be said that they were made
for each other.

And what of the "child" of this marriage, Albert Peggs? He is
both the recipient of Millicent's money, memories, and orders, and
"the lover of the spiritual world of Elijah Thrush." He is often
ordered to kneel, has seizures, feels ill, even thinks he is going mad.
He is a sponge who takes in everything the white people urge on
him, including their own projections of his blackhood; at the same
time, while he absorbs he exudes, as any pressed sponge will, and
there is a constant flowing of liquid out of his body—sweat, foam
—just as he is drinking in, however unwillingly, his new surround-
ings. And it must be emphasized that there is a very specific
contemporary relevance here. Albert is the black who has lost his
Southern self, and is as yet unable to find a new self in the North.
He is mythologized by the whites, but that is not the same thing as
rendering him an identity. In his position he is very vulnerable, and
it is part of his fate to be swamped in projections which prema-
turely deform what is as yet his unformed self. If he is the
inheritor he is also the victim; it may be "his period," but coming
into his "inheritance" is not an unambiguous privilege. At the wed-
ding of his surrogate parents, Albert can no longer remember his
name, which would indicate the final loss of whatever there was to
the original Albert Peggs. His final declaration, "I am Elijah
Thrush" is a crucial act of renomination and at the same time his
final self-annihilating act of obedience to white impositions. In the
alchemy of the book, is black transformed into gold? Or, more
sinisterly, is black forcibly turned into white? It could be that
Albert, having been emptied out, is by the end filled up with Elijah
Thrush—the host turned into the parasite. But perhaps he does it
for love.

Millicent admits that "we were not the right people" to "bring Albert out," but she insists that he had to come out sometime. Again, near the end, Elijah insists that "we've boarded the wrong ship." Just so Fenton Riddleway, in 63: Dream Palace, says with sudden panic: "Do you think we're really in the right house maybe?" Wrong house, wrong ship, wrong parents—to many of Purdy's bereft and wandering figures, such apprehensions are only aspects of a larger terror, that of having fallen into the wrong world, which, however, is the only world there is. If there is an intermittent feeling that this is the wrong world, it is not surprising that we should be able to detect the recurrence of a distinct onto-logical anxiety or uncertainty—particularly in Albert who has no place in this world and thus no self.

But in addition to being about the problems of relationships, America, the family, identity, perhaps most importantly the book is about language. Purdy's work is full of all kinds of narrators, writers, fabricators, confabulators, memoirists, all in different ways either trying to ensnare the reality of another person's life in words, or compelled to undertake the listening and writing task, or actually attempting to evoke some reality to fill in the dark pits of their ignorance. As often as not, the reality these people are after eludes their words and vanishes into the unreachable silence of absence or death. To be born is to be inserted into a particular discourse, which to a large extent will determine the values, modes of percep-tion, formulations of reality, by which and in which we live. And quite as often as feeling that they are in the wrong house, Purdy's central figures feel that they are in the wrong language. Thus Albert, a reluctant memoirist, finds that the words poured into him radically change his consciousness (some of his lapses from consciousness may be attributed to a surfeit of the wrong words). As he realizes from the start, once he has met Elijah Thrush he starts "falling into his. . . . language"; and here is a more important statement: "More than anything else. . . . the money, the humiliation, the hate of this great house where I was a paid memoirist, it was the language spoken which was now becoming mine that made me go out of my head." There are different forms of enslavement, and black Albert has been taken over, his mind both narcotized and manacled, by an alien language. To say that as a narrator he hardly sounds like a black person is not enough: the point is that he sounds like no person at all. Albert discovers that Millicent and Elijah "often

employed the identical favorite phrases, words, idioms." To the
extent that Albert accepts being absorbed into this surrogate family,
he has to accept that language, so that the narrator and the nar-
rated come to share and sustain a curious many-layered discourse
characterized by archaic gentilities, abrupt formalities, exaggerated
politeness, unexpected fragments of the vernacular and colloquial,
ritualized abuse, splenetic irritability, unprovoked imperiousness,
obscuring pedantries—and sudden helpless cries of yearning, need,
pain, and love. If Albert can say "as you done promised me" in
traditional darky dialect, he can also shout out "Cunctator of
cuntators," a positively Nabokovian lexical obscurity (it means
"delayer"). He is full of words but has no language to call his own,
employing instead the synthetic language of those around him. It is
one more paradox that Albert's linguistic confusion, or inherited
eclecticism, is also Purdy's stylistic triumph.

There is one further aspect to the existence of the weird, dis-
sonant speech of the book, a speech as deracinated as the speakers.
One statement from Millicent points directly to it. Thus she ad-
dresses the Bird of Heaven: "But be glad, my angel, you can't talk.
Your affliction is your happiness. It's talking that has made man
lower than the brutes of creation, and is God's most calamitous
mistake from which all other mistakes stem. Had the beast never
talked, this would be a fairer, greener place, and history, that
parched synthetic middling bore of a nightmare, which is eating
away even at my brains, would never have been." Her pessimisms
and exhaustion are her own, but it is a truism that without speech
there would be no culture, history, consciousness—or books. Purdy
himself uses words brilliantly, and it is only an apparent paradox
that one of the main feelings in his work is that talk is our torment;
that is, it torments us with the illusion of communication, while
obscuring or distorting what we have to say. It may also take the
place of emotion, or serve as a powerful tool in using people as
things to implement one's own schemes. How much better to be
unconsciously in nature, singing like a bird, instead of being
trapped in language and as Conrad put it "out of life—utterly out
of it": or, if we can't regress to a prelingual state, then to transcend
language, entering the heaven-haven of silence. These are not
Purdy's specific conclusions but meditations provoked by the book.
Looked at another way, the book accepts that man, like a Beckett
character, will go on muttering to the end, dreaming of a bird song

lost and a silence yet to be reached. But then this book does so many things, finally resisting demystification through its inexhaustible magic. It gives us the words, the bird song behind the words, and the silence around them, a silence which is not a void but a total repletion of meaning.

FOUR POEMS

ROBERT NICHOLS

THE MEANING OF FESTIVALS

1

A ray of sun breaks thru the clouds & illuminates
a field   And I am surrounded by light as if coming
from the white birches   or the snow on the ground/
thru which stalks of goldenrod lift up

weeds & the flowering crowns of ferns
                touched with radiance
It is the meaning of the festivals revealed
so long hidden . . .

the brown skeletons of the ferns   the flute sounds
her cheek smeared with turmeric paste shines
                                yellow yellow
As the dancer raises her eyes to me
                the river of time stops

2

The swirling street   Animals
crowds of people in costumes, masks
the dream spirals with the drum beat   in the heat
the revellers are throwing colored powder at each other

                    By the bank of the sacred river
the throng bathes   wedged against itself

As in the old story: A shout
"The bulls have been stolen   the royal doors
to the cattle shed have been broken into." We must follow
the thieves thru the suburbs   under the banner of
                        the "Right Communists"
thru the mists of time

Firecrackers explode   the marchers have broken into a run
in front of the governor's mansion in Calcutta. My eyes
swim. We're backed to the curb. A procession of lanterns
the crowd separates & a cart is pulled thru slowly decorated
with flowers the bride preceded by a limousine.

Her veil is the mystery.
The bulls are loose on the street
The crush deepens. The radio blares out
that the municipal power plant has been sabotaged

3
This is the way DEIR is performed:
on the day before: fast
        wash away the chaff from the threshing floor
        sweep the shrine   Women leave the lights on
        and go to the rooftop with your pitchers
        and pour out water to the moon

On the morning of DEIR:
        by this time the fireplace has been replastered
        the house machinery has been oiled and the tools put away
        The children may go around in groups begging for toys
        The Ganji Figure (tantra) has been incised on the wall
            in fresh plaster

At 2 p.m. or an appropriate time:
        the Household gathers and the story of Ganji is told
            Ganji—the Speedy One

Each time a part of the story is completed one of
  the family shouts
and the storyteller drops in a bean
When the pot is full of beans the story is ended.

The complete mantra for Ganji-Devi:

```
devi   devi   devi   GA
                              sa bu    thanoi
devi   devi   GA
DEvi   devi   ga
OM   sabu   thanoi   om   ga
WEE   HA
WEE   HA
OOO   ri   ai   GAI   ba
              WEE   HA
              WEE   HA
OOO   ri   ai   GAI   SABU   THANOI
GA   OO   OM   SABU   SABU   THANOI   BA
              WEE   BA
              WEE   BA
DEvi   devi   ga
RAmi   devi   ga
RAmi   RAmi   BA
DEvi   ba
```

    "BE IN GOOD HEALTH!"
    (or a better translation:
   may there be good public health)

4
The meaning of the festivals is revealed
    as the snow melts from the hill
bare patches of the earth
the stiff heads of weeds still up and flying
     their pennants
leftovers of the year
    the Festival

And the long line of cars going out bumper to bumper
     "City traffic   it's awful   but it'll ease soon
                    as we reach the pike"
Headlights of the cars sweep the nite
the children asleep in the back seat
                in their best clothes
"Going to visit grandmother
              for the Holidays"

Wheels
the whole country on the move
            worshiping the GOD

Sing it!
"a poem is no more than a pair of tight pants"
      Frank ("Francis") O'Hara
killed Fire Island Atlantic sands
         June 1961
by jeep taxi
           ebb tide of the breath
Death among the sea shells

5
GODDESS MOTHER MATTA PROTECT US FROM CHOLERA
                   PROTECT US FROM SMALL-
                   POX
                   PROTECT US FROM POWER
                   FAILURES
                   PROTECT US FROM
                   BACTERIA MUTATIONS
GODDESS MOTHER MATTA PROTECT US FROM SNAKE
                   BITE
                   PROTECT US FROM TRAFFIC
                   ACCIDENTS
      BLOOD ON THE HIGHWAY (Mike's & Jeanie's—WHY?)
     SIV—RATTRI OF THE MIRACULOUS MEDAL
                   PROTECT US FROM
                   THE WEATHER
PROTECT US SIV RATTRI MOTHER OF SULPHUR

Walking thru the fields this March day/   & the meaning of
the festivals is made clear
where it was hidden

skies like a blue tide
woods purple
bare spots of ochre grass and raw sienna earth
showing thru

squirt of mud   under my boots
eternal return of the time
Seasons of the earth/   sainte terre/   holy land
sauntering thru the country

6

MENSAS—A CALENDAR

PHAGUN	SIVRATTRI	weather changes
(Feb. March)		worship of refrigerator
CAIT	KRI	ghi lamps are lit
(May)	RARALI	the child gets his first haircut
SAVAN	TIJ	swings hung from the trees
(July)		wrestling & menstruating exercises
ASAUJ	KANAGAT	Allhallows eve
(Oct.)		when the dead come back
POH	MAKAR	quarrels are patched up
(Nov. Dec.)	SANKRANT	policemen's motorcycles are decorated
MAGH	BASANT	Grandfather Frost's day
(Feb.)	PANCAMI	last bags of rice are given away

"Tij comes and sows the seeds of the festivals
Holi takes them away and wraps the Festivals in her shawl

and so the year passes

and so the year passes

7
In the heat of the courtyard   we are gathered this Amavas day

my brothers have swept the ground bare
                in the newness of this holiday

& made the effigy on the wall
on the matrix of the brite whitewashed wall
                        on this the fifth day

our buttermilk into Ganji's mouth
Our hands fashioning the picture out of cowdung:
                MANKIND'S head and mouth

Sing the festival song:
                on this the fifth day
        "GRANDMOTHER   COWDUNG WEALTH
            BE WITH US!
        from the necks the four walls of our house extended into
            the landscape"

contains us and the sacred animals
                blessed be this Easter of the year
We fashion it out of straw
                the model of the Celestial City

Weeds flame
                the head of goldenrod burns

FEAST MY BROTHERS

THE FOUR STAGES

                        (*for Franz Fanon: once a poet
                then doctor serving with the Algerian Liberation Army*)

Franz   I can't say my life is not changed
Franz   correct me
                if these aren't the four stages of the journey
        you made for both of us

1

A village buzzing with flies
the bus at Colombe-Bechar
        waits for the peasants with their baskets of chickens
We leave the dusty square
    journey by steamship from Algiers to Marseilles
the wonderful ride by night
        orchards of the French countryside lighted up
in the beam of the locomotive   train with its wheels
    its electrified switches   turbines
glides into Paris
                        Dawn
Franz   that trainride is worth
    40,000 years of African history

Village of Colombe-Bechar buzzing with flies
        the dry palm leaves clatter against each other
the children are throwing sticks
There is a massacre at Retif   which we don't hear about
450 Algerians slaughtered by the gendarmes

At Oud-i-waka   at the quarries
the machine guns have cut down a hundred prisoners
but we don't think about it
        Only
about our escape!
We can't wait
                        as the bus pulls out

        our hearts leap

2

In Paris we became humanists
you with your black dick
I with my flint eyes and bone knuckles
        We became Greeks

Franz   you've had nothing to eat for three days
only the economies of John Stuart Mill
        and the theories of Liebknecht and Auguste Comte

the greenhouse of culture steams
Our voices have condensed
        in drops
    against the hot panes of glass
        of the Jardin des Plantes

WORDS!

Franz   what has happened to us?
  we've flipped out   dissolved into the European bloodstream
with your thick lips pursed around the words
            As if you were eating peppers
you have schooled yourself to speak
            the pure couplets of Heredia

Franz!
  how many cups of coffee have we consumed
in the café off Rue M. le Prince
drenched in the light of these silver candelabra?

But you are brought back to who you are
by the clatter of metal   a beggar at the curb
        rummaging thru the garbage can
You remember you are not white

3
This is the stage where you Play the Nigger
            like you say Franz
as we in New York are making it with High Camp
up goes the priest's frock at mass
with a carrot up his ass
labelled "George Washington sucks"

we scandalize them in the name of the common humanity
            POVERTY
                    is the only obscenity

I ask you:
Follow the child uphill
towards the barriada with its tin roofs
          La Paz Lima
she has filled her pail at the last city hydrant

and the boy walking down the road
with the dead rabbit under his coat (that Neruda describes)
               As the car of the rich man passes
          his eyes turn to two stones

In all of the rotten slums   Watts Newark
                    Algiers
Dakar Brazzaville Johannesburg Bogota Capetown
the children beg for bread
the women are selling themselves
and the men have become pimps and police spies

Your brothers and sisters

     Franz   there is nothing else to do but dance and make fun
Franz   you have tossed away your scholarship
You have demolished your bowler hat
and kicked off your Italian leather shoes
ba-ruum ba- ruum ba- ruum
you dance barefoot in the dust
banging your ass as a drum
you have used the sun for an earring
& rattled your gold teeth

          "Playing the Nigger"

4
So we have reached the 4th Stage
when the children on the road
          are saying to you
     STOP MAKING POEMS

While we are dancing
          they have arrived to watch us: the sightseers

a busload of black real-estate operators out of Dakar
they clap and throw pennies at our feet
                              Disgusting

Franz   Franz   who do you think you reach with your
        dusty dance
Franz   who do you want watching you?
            who do you want listening to you?

Think: the boy with the stone eyes
                              walking down the road
does he suddenly come to you   and light up?
does his face change?
And the whore waiting at the street corner
        her ear to the transistor radio
turned in to your music?   Is she purified?

In the forlorn suburbs of Africa shacks with the corrugated
      tin roofs
                        put together out of old crates
a moth loops by the streetlamp   in the hut
the whole family lies asleep on the mud floor
It's dark   and is it your song
                that breaks thru the roof?

And the laborer who has worked all day for the white planter
he lies in the barracks on the wet pallet
                        his back scarred

Does your song heal the welts?

NO!   LIES!   LIES!

THEY ARE NOT LISTENING TO YOU

Franz
From the square at Colombe-Bechar comes the dry rattle of
      machine guns
Take it!
the Angel of Silence stuffs his fist into your mouth

THE FURNACE TENDER

Skrugg came into the plant when he was trained   and he
stayed there. There was another percussion under the
roof than the one he knew. It was different from the percussion
agitating the street   from the one agitating
his own blood.

Sometimes the foreman stood behind him red in the face
and sometimes they shared a coffee thermos together
on the bending grid outside the forge.

The red eye of the forge flamed and flamed. Skrugg
watched it steadily with the same eyes as he watched the
shambling men on the streets   the men in his own
neighborhood that he knew were not working

Fuel slipped through the pipes—pale viscous fuel
diesel metered into the furnace by Skrugg. And when
it came it flamed and the beams ballasted inside the
furnace bloomed and bloomed

Pale amber colored diesel   bars passing from their white
climax to calibrations of rose   to rose-plum   to purple
Crane shuttling between the shop and the yard   crane
hoisting the hard plates with its magnet of charged ions
Skrugg watched the steel plates come into the plant and go
and the men come and go.

The plant had three eyes   the foreman's eye
the furnace's eye   and Skrugg's eye. Of these three
Skrugg's was the steadiest

Sometimes from the air   sometimes from the air over
the harbor   there came a curved lovely sound.
It fell like a whip through the window. It flaked off
the grey scales from the steel he had cooked
It hammered against his eyes   and softened Skrugg's
own backbone so that he almost had to cry to himself
Enough   enough

THE MAN WHO SOLD MAHATMA GANDHI
LIFE INSURANCE

he was a you wd expect   an american
who had operated successfully out of Des Moines
                              Omaha & Tulsa
& who came 9500 miles to the City of Bombay
where he just happened to catch Gandhi
while he was having lunch
                              & sold him

a complete policy health security retirement coverage for life
& thereinafter redeemable   his beneficiaries . . .
all for the sum of . . .
at that time a rupee . . .
being worth a half dollar . . .

Homer P. Hogsbristle   what have you done?
        Ace salesman of the Mutual of Omaha

you have subverted the first saint of the Twentieth Century
a man whose lungs are directly inflamed
                              with the breathing of God
whose wife is folded   in the half-flexed knee-joint of God
whose children are on the eyelid of God

        "He sweet-talked me" Gandhi remarked in a news
interview some weeks later   when he had cancelled his insurance
        "If he'd come anytime earlier
I'd never have had all that money in my pocket.
If he'd come afterwards   I wouldn't have been interested"

Oh no   Guru
then

                        you'd have been fasting
                        you wd have been spinning
                        you wd have been way way way way out
                                    making salt

But consider this occult salesman
from Omaha   with his home-made product
how he came 9000 miles & sold it
to the least likely man on the whole earth
at exactly the right time

                    & if that isn't
a real act of american Black Magic I'll eat my hat

EIGHT POEMS

ROBERT MORGAN

BLACKBERRIES

Among the bloodfilled eyes
and towering vegetation,
an invisible
traffic of chiggers.
Leaves bear ticks like hungry berries.
Dive in trampling mole runs
and spilling birdnests,
brush the fanged stems
to gather a few
with the bluejays and yellow jackets.
Wade into the snaky weeds as into a mine field.
Leaves have caught in the briars
and piled up a hive for rats
and spiders.
Quail leave in a snort.
The arching long necked thickets
are weighted with loads of shot
bright as caviar.

BLUE RIDGE

The divide is sharp as a mule's bony back,
parts rainfall at the rim
and forwards it on.
The decision made here.
Higher separate peaks flank
the defining ridge, but it wanders
unbroken, wind plucked,
running out
through mists and rhododendron,
above hemlocks and dripping ledges.
The soaked ground discharges
like a battery
current of clear water.
Here a spring has first choice,
is the first gathering of moisture, a valve
feeding out evenly
far from the sweet thrusting
into estuaries, the sloughs of rich
chemistry
and dissipation in tidal flats.
Here is no accumulation.
At the farthest boundary
of the ocean's magnetic field
water gathers itself from
the dirt speaking cold and clear.

LAND DIVING

Though it's no disgrace to refuse
some things must be done.
And present accomplishment
is no guarantee
of future.
You must come close
as possible without touching
to prove brinksmanship, fly
from the sapling girdered tower

before the whole village, leaping with a scream
against the wall of fear, step onto
the white-hot floor
of emptiness
holding only to yourself.
You will know the pure isolation of fall.
The vines bound to your feet must not snag
on the scaffolding
or they will swing you crushing
into the frame and braces.
They must not break
or be an inch too long
or you will be smothered by
the swat of earth.
Yet the meaning is the closeness.
You cannot stretch out your arms;
you must be jerked to a stop face against
the trampled dirt
by the carefully measured
bonds.
Only they can save you.

PUMPKIN

By fall the vines have crawled out
twenty yards from the hill, threading the tall grass
and coiling under weeds.
The great cloth leaves have shrivelled
and fallen. No sign of a harvest.
No way to tell where the pumpkins are scattered.
Except to wade into the briars and matted grass,
among hornet nests and snakes,
parting the brush
with a hoe. Or wait
a few weeks longer till the weeds dry
up, burned by frost,
and the huge beacons
shine through
like planets submerged and rising.

HOLLYHOCK

Aims a blast from its chalky core
and draws the dart
shot from an unseen blowgun.
The hummingbird scores
and stings
humming. Needles the white
and is repelled, held out frozen
and drawn back, stabbing and probing
the long nipple, punctures
and drinks,
chipping from the bull's-eye
fragments of seed that fall into
the closing fist
and the target drops off rotting immediately.

VOICE

The pine filters song from the wind
creating
shadows and dopplers
of obstruction,
slicing music from the open
flow, causing the air
to reflect and refract against itself.
But a greater
resonance
is made by tying off
a knot of its motion in an eddy,
a swirl inside the mouth of bottle or cave,
filling and inflating
the belly,
neck and lips,
and the urn or skull,
egg or hollow tree, glows
with sound
though broken and empty
as the brainless walnut shell.

ELECTRICAL STORM

At the blackhot core of day
the head lifts
over the cool ridge
advancing
a niagara wide as the sky.
Comes raking the mountains with white claws
draining. Oceans
pour over the approaching
front. The earth is struck like a drum
and swept by darkness,
plowed ground still hot.
A cold tide washes.
Straight overhead
cliffs and geysers topple.
Above the black barges and pilings
of rain, above the grinding floes and crumbling
towers. Above it all high snow forests
glide in the sun.

SHRINE

Icicles put heads out
of the cracks in the cliff and drive
through from inside the mountain.
Roots flatten
over the cliff face
stretching tendons of water.
Holding the great molars and tusks.
Sperm grows
tallowing columns
of a vast portico at the mountaintop.
Burning thousands of candles at sunrise.
Steam blows from inside the cave.
At thaw the pillars
topple
leaving the cliff's bare face.

THE KEEPSAKE

COLEMAN DOWELL

I told Beatrix "Yes!" gladdened to think that her friendliness, and Jeremiah's, apparently, had carried over the fall separation; it was at least plain that enough of our summer feeling remained for them to want to come to me at the farm for Christmas, and for me to want them. After we hung up, following mutual assurances that none of us could really wait (Jeremiah, too; Beatrix spoke for him), I checked the dates she had given me, inclusive only of mystery when she spoke, and found that they encompassed a week. I was accustomed to winter guests coming on the Eves of things and departing the day after The Day; the thought of someone willing to endure for a longer time touched me.

I have determinedly never set my cap for younger people, so the youngness of the Dresdens was an incidental in our success with each other, as I suppose my comparative oldness was. Granted that some of the most successful things we did together could be called "young" things: flying kites in my fields among the cropping sheep; sailing too far too late in the day, being bested for hours by the tide at the harbor mouth, the day sailor flapping to the dock at midnight like an exhausted bird . . . but I do these things on my own with just my dachshund bitch for company.

Incidental, too, I suppose, was that the three of us, roughly, shared a profession: Jeremiah, poet; Beatrix, novelist; and I a more or less failed playwright: my very long-running (five years) play in Germany is to American recognition as sound waves from that falling unheard tree to ears.

88

When we met at the ferry slip, introduced by my dachshund, Miss Gold, what we knew of each other was what we had surmised those several Fridays in succession, seeing each other waiting for the train-ferry. I had made no effort to find out who they were; I have been here long enough to say to myself "summer people" and let the description suffice. They were interesting looking, he classically handsome, she as ugly as an ape until one saw through to her simian but real beauty. I had seen through to it before we met; had seen through Jeremiah, too, or thought that I had; his niceness seemed both glass and shield. As we said, my house guests and I, passing judgment sometime in midsummer after several exposures to the Dresdens, Jeremiah was surely the kindliest poet, too nice to be really great, perhaps . . . Among the judges was a poet of enduring reputation, so maybe the consensus was partly satirical.

Concerning the Dresdens knowing "who" I was before we met, people generally can find out my identity by giving one of three clues to any passer-by: the car, the only foreign one on the Island; Miss Gold, whose photograph adorned the cover of a collection (*Coursing*) of my plays; or any word at all of my own appearance, which is eccentric, especially among the plain-groomed Islanders and summer people who are not groomed at all.

But as I have said, Miss Gold introduced us, I don't think in complicity with Beatrix and Jeremiah, though if they had wanted to meet me, cultivating Miss Gold was the best way to go about it.

I mean through these "incidentals" to set up vibrations of suspicion, of the possibility of a kind of fortune hunting. I will go farther and say that my house is the only one on the island where any kind of fortune hunting is possible, and let the matter rest there; we are all adventurers and if vibrations are at this juncture misleading, then let us call the story a "mystery" and, through a glass, darkly, look for clues.

Beatrix's telephone call gave me two weeks' notice, and in those two weeks I accomplished more than I would ordinarily have done in a month. Before she called, my only guest was to be my best friend, the poet mentioned in the foregoing, who is this year's lion as he was last year's lion and my sole Christmas guest. Paul and I are too relaxed with each other for me to go to any real pains against his visits, but for the Dresdens the house was cleaned and rooms were opened.

In allusive tribute there would be a German Christmas dinner: goose and sauerkraut in Riesling and potatoes sauteed in goose fat and thick applesauce domed with its own jelly. My yearly gift from the smokehouse of home, an aged Kentucky ham, could open the meal with Madeira-steeped figs; there would be custards and spiced beef and pork pie in a crust and plum pudding. To this extent is a host allowed, sorcererlike, to meddle with the future: the Dresdens would be flattered by the German motif, and Paul, a secret Pip, would be pleased by the Dickens touches.

But early on Christmas Eve morning Paul called; early, he said, to prove that he had got up in time to make the train . . . but. He is usually precise, admirably so to a discursive person like me, but I did not get much past the "but"; in any case he was not coming. He was not especially sorry; he knew that I would not be alone. I had not told him about the Dresdens; it seemed that they themselves had told him. It also seemed blatantly like a clue, but to what I could not· imagine. Paul had liked Beatrix, with whom he had in common Brooklyn, an Eastern band I have found to be as strong as a wedding ring. He liked Jeremiah's poetry, liked his looks; as he put it, he even liked Jeremiah, when he remembered him.

Paul is not a cruel man, nor is he unusually just; he is mainly disinterested, and I had to admit that the précis was accurate of many an essay of Jeremiah. His lack of temperament, of eccentricity, of vice, apparently, bleached him out; too frequently one gazed at the place where Jeremiah was without seeing him.

When one said, or wrote down, "the Dresdens," it was Beatrix's simianity that gave proper flesh to the noun; Jeremiah was an essence, flushing the tissue with blood, coursing, undoubtedly healthily, out of sight; but as we forget our blood until we are cut, so did we lose sight of Jeremiah. A quip about his combination of vivid looks and colorless personality—"Beside him, other men pale to significance"—was not successful because of his art, which *was* significant, rather Augustinian. If, as some maintained, he was a throwback, it was to the best traditions.

His lovely ape wife could never approach his art. Her own was imitative of Nathalie Sarraute, experimental of many things but never emotion. But in person she was dark emotional energy, faintly furred (in silhouette against light she wore an aureole, the filaments of fuzz glowing uniformly). She gave the impression, in the electricity of life, of teetering on the edge of breakdown, or breakthrough, some volatile display or discovery a nod away, waiting only for her permissive recognition. One both longed for and feared the revelation of Beatrix.

Their visibility, or lack of it; their art or attempts *manqués;* these are further incidentals as such extraneous matters always are in love and lust. They had won my allegiance and revived the intensity of long-dormant curiosity about others, and I don't know how they did it. Jeremiah could have been ectoplasm, Beatrix entirely without talent, and their effect upon me would have been the same. It is hindsight that tells me so, for I write from a knowledge of worse than pallor and pretentiousness, and still curiosity, if not allegiance, persists.

They called from the island side of the ferry, and Miss Gold and I drove through immensely billowing curtains of snow to pick them up and welcome them with champagne in the car. They were swathed like papooses as though we were a Canadian outpost, great dark sunglassed eyes all that Miss Gold and I could see of them, both of us lightly clad in sweaters in the snow-warm air.

In a story by Beatrix the focus, endlessly circled, would be the hidden eyes, the muffled mouths; they would become the characters, the only physical properties referred to, and because they were hidden, thus missing, slowly we would realize that Beatrix's story was about two pairs of sunglasses, two scarves, incapable of emotion but possessing a curious molecular ability to deduce, finally to murder through subtraction . . . Simple behavior, catching at her imagination like a fishhook, could cause her to darken with visible passion and pain and her fingers to crook as though tearing in retaliation great laden chords from her typewriter.

I am more concerned with what can be barely intuited, with those actions and reasons explainable only by atavism, accessible only to instinct. I am not interested in the cult of game playing or the psychology behind the way people sit or hold their cigarettes, and this indifference to gesture, to the visual, actually, makes me rather an odd playwright. But concerning the Dresdens' appearance, whatever their wish may have been for concealment, they were thin-blooded city people with smog-weakened eyes; and it was soon apparent that Jeremiah had a very bad case of laryngitis; his voice was a ragged thread fraying further with the slightest use. What to make of this new effacement: Jeremiah become his

Art entirely? . . . That is me still being Beatrix; it is not my style at all.

The Dresdens were grateful for the warmth of the car. The train had been bitterly cold. They remembered with pleasure the snugness of my house, the first fire, bright on the hearth (Beatrix, lyrical), that we had shared in late September. Did I seem to be protesting her memory when I said, hating to, that the north wind changes things? Sometimes, I said, it pulls the heat out of the house and makes it hard to maintain a temperature much above 68°. But there are fireplaces—

Indifferently, I thought, Beatrix inquired how Paul was holding up under the cold. At my news the air in the car changed.

Miss Gold's reactions always engage me more than my own, and I watched her sensing the change, lifting her nose high and sniffing soundlessly. I have seen her smell my anger before it broke, and dishonesty in others when the dishonesty was, as it would turn out, ripe with consequences. But she does not draw conclusions and frequently I cannot; though I thought that the changed air was colder.

Jeremiah must go instantly to bed there to be fed with honey and lemon and comforted with hot-water bottles and judicious visits. But Beatrix made a trip to their apartment and came down blue and trembling, asking if they possibly could sleep by the fire. In alarm, thermometer in hand, I went up cursing the wind, felt somewhat cooler than the rooms when I discovered a uniform temperature of 74°, infernal for my house in winter. Beatrix, I thought, is being womanly; women hate, so I have found, to be thought hardy, even when too stony to be chipped from. I recalled that she shivered a great deal on the stillest summer nights, gathering to herself the garments of others, and I amended my thought to: Beatrix is being Beatrix.

I built the fire up to a roar (Beatrix, as I went to the kitchen: "Isn't he afraid of chimney fires?") and went to put the kettle on for tea, feeling in the second person like a domestic. I told myself (on paper; that day warranted three journal entries) that champagne, of which I had drunk a lot, being two thirds bubbles is two thirds fancy. Winter adjustment to summer friends, I wrote, leads to suspicion, is trying of our resources, is frequently sad, frequently abandoned. Remember, I wrote, who these people are. Were.

Here is Beatrix:

Beatrix, asking what something cost; Beatrix, requesting the salt cellar (it's onion soup, not salt soup). Her voice seemed to have got higher since summer and had acquired a habit of repeating what one was saying *under* what one was saying—not quite simultaneously, but as close-tailing as an afterbeat in music. If spoken words were visible, then talking with Beatrix would be like speaking above a mirror. But her charm grew apace, too, and by early nightfall she had woven a screen to block out nearly all her minor transgressions.

She and Jeremiah napped by the fire, she under a favorite winterthing of Miss Gold's, a robe of South American rabbit in white and various browns, beautiful as vicuña. I took it out to her on impulse as she lay with her spread hair seeming to grow like ivy on the blue velvet cushions. In the firelight she and Jeremiah looked exotic, dark-haired, both of them, and swart. Beatrix rubbed the fur vigorously as though frictionally to disclose its nature. The fur was like her own pelt; the rubbing made her seem to be looking for fleas or salt deposits. Unconsciously I had abetted the ape in her. Jeremiah, bent in his chair, stirred as though to question my propriety. But no, the shape he assumed in the chair was more commalike.

I turned on the Christmas lights. In the glowing room, fire fallen to embers, the Dresdens looked like young dreamers in a ballet. Each sleeping profile thrust upward, carving out the wine-jelly Christmas sheen of the room. They were perfectly strange to me, characterless as people sleeping on a stage when the curtain goes up. Dimly felt tendrils ran from my breast to summer and turned back and groped for the Dresdens but did not touch them, restrained by my desire. If I had thought Beatrix vulgar today, it was *had* thought; this woman was a sleeping woman, no more. And if I had thought whatever I had thought about Jeremiah since arrival—not much, to be truthful—I thought nothing of the sort about the sleeping man. As a result, perhaps, the evening was a lute tuned perfectly to our *accordatura*. The visit was saved, all was redeemed, reputations, judgments, friendliness, love—all saved. There is a relief like shock; the difference is that one must help the relief to voluntary numbness: third journal entry of the day with "clarify" in the margin. I never did.

Early morning scrambling, tissue paper, trailing ribbons leading, like false clues, radially outward from the tree through doorways. Was the tree then the beast?

The presents were fine: A kite sculpture in memoriam; Paul's wonderful new fantasy book in which, in disguise, Miss Gold and I figured; the silk scarves; the flowered set of mugs for the kitchen; new Mahler recordings, the unfinished Tenth Symphony underscoring the morning; sweaters, raincoats, carcoats for Miss Gold; Italian bottles of milk bath for everyone, and pomanders.

A box of fancy chocolates for Beatrix; her look of disbelief was fascinating. She put them on a table where they remained untouched throughout the visit, and where they were left when Beatrix had gone. No mystery, now; no point in making one out of it. That night, late, in a tense discussion about Women's Liberation, Beatrix brought up the chocolates, tossed them figuratively at my head: Would I give a man a box of chocolates? Would I want to see a male placidly stuffing himself on heart attacks and hardened arteries, chocolate death dribbling down his chin onto his—I interjected "Slim volume of poetry?" looking to Jeremiah for lightness; none forthcame. I said I hoped my chocolate-eating protagonist would be neat enough not to dribble hardened arteries.

Trembling like a wire, Beatrix reminded me that a man could eat with both hands, could smear himself with food and belch and undo buttons and pick his teeth—other things, too, of course; Beatrix had a liberated tongue. I did not know if I was being allowed a glimpse of formative years. I was momentarily confused, thinking that we had through the chocolates reverted to our discussion of calories, the only topic at dinner: Beatrix had estimated that if each of us had one helping of everything on my encomium-intended menu we would have swallowed 25,000 calories apiece. Jeremiah, placidly eating, had been laconic: "Stuff a cold" . . . But we were not discussing calories at all; calories did not matter. According to Beatrix, all that mattered was that I and others like me readjust our thinking and attitudes, by surgery if necessary, until the sight of Woman behaving exactly like Man under any and all circumstances would be no more objectionable than if it *were* a man.

For the first time between us, my age was mentioned: Beatrix thought it a factor, perhaps *the* factor, in my inflexibility. There was more but I did not attend too closely.

I retain an impression of Beatrix stoutly defending Doris Lessing, though not of anyone attacking her. Had this been Beatrix, in the summer, requiring no offensive to launch a defensive? It seemed a clue to her, an important one—as my age has turned out to be to me. Perhaps she believed that all were guilty until cleared by her offices.

I have acquaintances who attend a sort of church—God figures vaguely—where they improve memories, learn, as they put it, to "relate," and where they study such as the elaborate system of inner antagonisms and reprisals against Self of which we everyone are composed. When a bad water skiing accident followed the failure of my play in New York, my friends were glad for me: the inner wound had had to be matched by an outer wound—the mind's insistence that the body share the pain—before balance was restored.

On my way to bed, having had my age inflicted upon me, I slid on a rug, and in flailing for balance I wrenched my vulnerable back. Beatrix, seeing me teetering, sprang up. As though she were in a nimbus, I saw her as the messenger come to remind me that I was purified again, inner and outer wounds nicely balanced.

Jeremiah spends the days in bed, forcing liquids. At intervals Beatrix brings various cups and mugs down and sets them on the piano, from whence I hobble them to the kitchen and wash them. Women's Liberation has many radii. Some resemble crutches.

Beatrix, returning from a long walk (in her absence Jeremiah futilely summoned with dull poundings; Miss Gold replied with growls; a metaphysical dialog), bright-cheeked and giving, said to me, "You really are too good to your friends," and it was a summer voice speaking, shocking my eyes to water. With Francesca I believe that happiness recalled in misery is the greatest pain, just as dwelling upon it is the greatest folly.

I, walking Miss Gold, am reminded of a drawing of a man approaching a house whose shape has been assumed or consumed by a woman. Beatrix by dint of anger and frustration had consumed the house; all seemed now to be of her flesh, and the flesh was increasingly rank. Her pallor, the greenish cast of her shadowed complexion, aroused in me the aversion one feels for a corpse; odors were supplied by association. I would pass her in rooms of my mind with pomander pressed to my nostrils. The afterodors of her milk baths were sour; she had sat too long bottled without being shaken or heated and was going bad under my nose. I thought that she, two years married, might be frustrated on account of Jeremiah's weakness, that it might be sexual frustration. I became obsessed with her frustration. I was pursued by it.

I would sit by the fire, I am sitting by the fire trying to put summer through myself again. I sit in the shambles of Christmas, among portents of a shattered winter. I do not recover from aborted love sooner than I would regain strength following the loss of an organ. Fear of pain and the boredom of repetitive convalescence had driven me to seek a burrow at last in the country and a companion in Miss Gold to make cozy the house of roots.

Beatrix's importuning voice on the telephone winds about summer recollections, changing their coloration through pressure at vital points:

Can it really be that she said about a play of mine in manuscript that she would never theretofore have suspected my erudition? or had she said intelligence, or was it education she had not suspected? I see the setting—the table, the company showing off for each other: someone had seen Kokoschka in Switzerland, Bellow had said to someone, someone had "discovered" William Gass; I heard her words in a lull, other words to lull and then the ones about me, my play; others hear her words—Yes, because Jeremiah(!) breaks in to say that he told his wife the reason my erudition (education, intelligence) does not show is because I am Southern. Beatrix professes not to understand. She says, amusingly (coarsely!) that what you know, if you are from Brooklyn, you let stick out all over you. I say—could I have said?—that in the South the only things it is all right to display are manners.

To my winter eyes, watching the summer scene, the little shrug Beatrix replies with is as blatant as a belch.

Another table, another evening, dinner in the garden: Beatrix and Jeremiah sitting lumpish and silent. Later, my reference to "my silent dinner party." Beatrix, defensively: "We were comfortably turned inward" . . . Do I say (did I say) that a dinner party is the last place to turn inward? No, nor had I made the fittingly cold remark about manners. There were, are, never "exchanges" between us in that sense; there was, is, only Beatrix and heedless

Jeremiah; and doting me. Was there not? Or had I hated them then too—then, but in the future; hated them, knowing how they *would* be, but loving them helplessly then? Or it is now I love them, helplessly?

I ask my journal what I meant. Did I mean that summer excess as seen in winter is another thing? Did I mean that in summer the self, camouflaged in permissiveness—looseness of sports, cocktail parties, sexual misalliances—recognized laxness as part of earned leisure? It's true that in winter, lacking universal permission and nature's profligate example, the true self shows as surely as galls, leaf-hid in summer, do on trees. I try, but cannot tell whether it is truth or erroneous assessment or Charlus-streak unsuspected that has ruined my Christmas and shocked my coming year. It becomes less and less accessible, retreats into being a parable of summer people and winter people, those races who visit each other's countries on off seasons. Paul is a winter person, pared down to his manners, the fat of summer extravagance always dieted away in time. I do not know what I am, but if I were a summer person I would kill myself by spring.

Miss Gold bit Beatrix in the following sequence of events. 1. Beatrix tries to coax Miss Gold to chase a ball, Miss Gold's expression of incredulity maddening to one untalented with drawing pen or camera. 2. Beatrix moves Miss Gold from her chair by the fire to one distant, taking the chair herself, though two others and a sofa stand empty. 3. Beatrix at dinner curtly refuses her hostess a morsel of food, saying "You've had your dinner, now let me have mine." I think Miss Gold bit Beatrix as punishment for unoriginality rather than for stinginess or bad temper. I have followed the course of events and predicted the bite to myself. At my small nod and half-smile Beatrix locks herself in such a vise of self-concern that I can hear the clink of iron on iron, iron device on iron flesh.

Beatrix, out of some perversity that recalled manners to her when they were not wanted, was generous in her assurances that she was not hurt, but she was. I, in fact, could see no recovery for her.

I fear Beatrix's edges, her serration. I am drunk before the fire; her sharpness increases as though to pierce my protection to the heart. Will the blurring liquidly run and harden to edges again? Ask Beatrix.

Drunk, I am a victim; but drunk, I cannot be victimized. I talk back. I suggest that they have pursued me because of the people I know. I suggest that Paul's absence has turned her monster and isolated Jeremiah in an upper chamber from whence Assumption is but a thought away. I suggest that Miss Gold and I are helpless babes and she, Medea. Jeremiah's cough from above sounds a warning: *Don't speak; Beatrix is suggestible.*

She cast about her for satisfactory or outrageous victims, strayed into unexplored territory, lit on mutual acquaintances whom she had met through me in the summer and whom she and Jeremiah had seen several times in the fall in town.

She demolishes reputations and characters; finished, I think; but she proves still hungry and tears the limbs from the couple's two children and goes on and eats the youngest, a boy of five. The illusion is astounding; Beatrix's mouth is gory and loops of saliva glisten in firelight. My skin blazes; the scarf she gave me for Christmas, ingratiatingly worn, touches me and burns. I tear it off.

Beatrix was aghast, unable to claim her words. It was, she said, as though she had been possessed. She begged for my belief, and I had no inclination after such excesses to doubt her. My willingness made Beatrix sullen; it was as though I had accused her.

With Miss Gold I nap secretly, tucked into a room I have shown to no one, a smoothly enclosed old inglenook unsuspected in the house's present symmetry, windowless as a womb. Do I hear her searching for me, calling, afraid of my escape? Do I hear him padding beside her, panting? Miss Gold's instincts lie still beneath sleep, her hackles consolingly quiescent. The smell from the useless fireplace is as fusty as Puritans. My house of roots, a long gallery of sensations more graphic than portraits. Their Puritan clothes, lye, ashes, leaching; leached of lies, from here one could emerge restored.

Jeremiah was in the yellow chair writing. As I came in he said "I think my wife has deserted my bed for yours" and went back to his writing.

In my bedroom Beatrix was in my bed, propped upon my pillows, under the fur robe. One glance shows stacks of books about her, a box of Kleenex, a bottle of pills. Used Kleenexes strew the floor, a rough path by which the wastebasket may be reached. There is a negligee over the back of the desk chair. It is like the onset of mystery, or like the very end of mystery: soon Jeremiah will come in, and the three of us . . . Beatrix and Jeremiah and I . . . Miss Gold, too? Jeremiah comes in. He wants to lie down. It seems that I should move aside so that he may join his wife. Somehow I cannot.

When Jeremiah had gone upstairs to nap Beatrix began. She mimicked voices, launching right in like a stand-up comic. Sometimes the voice was clear, at other times there was interference as though the sound were projected over water. The voice would be recognizable—Paul's, mine—and then not at all, though the words would seem to have been plucked from one's mind yesterday. Paul was excoriated, I berated; summer words reappeared in new contexts. A formidable writer, she could have been, serving imagination and total recall, if she were not so pretentious as to be blind to her own gifts.

I heard my voice through the medium of Beatrix saying hateful things about Women's Liberationists, deploring women writers using dirty words; uncannily, my voice in Beatrix's throat said that a prurient attitude seemed to be growing among female writers, and it gave specimens; it had been a good year for proof; then Beatrix's voice corrected my pronunciation by example: I, she said, don't think women are at all pure-ient; her rebuttal as unfelicitous as her correction. I half expected Miss Gold, tucked uneasily under a corner of the fur robe, to bite Beatrix for sloppiness. Pathetically, one charged and countered in the person of Beatrix; and one listened.

The telephone rang. My back twanged like a guitar string. Jeremiah's step was heard on the stair. All at once separate strings of a final knot place themselves at our fingertips.

As though the devoured child's father had by divine intervention been able to substitute himself for his child, he had died in the early morning. Our maligned acquaintance, even as Beatrix savaged him and his family, had lain dead . . . Had lain dying? It was a formidable weapon for Paul to hand me at such a time.

I listened to his voice that touched death with reason. The widow had asked him to help her make calls; the word was only that the dead man had (in his wife's recalled Viennese accent) died in sleep, for which we could all be grateful; "He had liked very much living." I wanted to shatter the quiet, to scream that Beatrix had killed him, that he had died in knowing horror . . . My acquaintance, or me?

Jeremiah, returning from the kitchen, gave me a look of surprise in passing. I wondered what my expression was like to give him such surprise. Carefully, perfectly aware of Beatrix listening, I inquired after "the little ones." Paul told me that the girl was fine, the boy, too, except that he expected to be allowed to keep his father's head.

"Don't" I said sharply. Paul understood. We said emotionally balanced goodbys. I retched dryly, keeping Beatrix waiting.

Beatrix leaned through a swarm or a gale that roiled her hair. *"What did you tell Jeremiah not to do?"* His mild presence behind me was like saneness. I stood aside to let him pass. What had she imagined had been going on between us? I was unable to duck the swarm of images, Beatrix's images surely of what had taken place out of her sightlines. I let the swarm take me. I believed that I knew what the lining of a mad mind looked like.

In the therapeutic tub I planned how I best might use my acquaintance's death. The dead, I told myself, don't mind how we use them. I shall not mind when I am dead how many Beatrixes to further themselves manipulate my bones. The dead don't mind. But words came: In death there is other sleep, other closing/Compared to which, death's dozing.

By the fireside they were still. Beatrix, unposed, stanceless, was disarmingly plain and young looking. Her reading glasses were askew, her mouth quirked. Her long arms reached the book out toward the hearth's light. A literate, uneasy ape. I could play on her vulnerability, catching her unawares with the news of death, the head; she would think that it was not the child she had devoured but the father, all but his head.

Jeremiah said that someone created his own light. Seeing Beatrix's look of sullenness at praise wasted on an absent someone, I thought "Poor man, your wife creates her own darkness."

By my bed I found my journal where Beatrix had left it. She had told me not to leave letters lying about, for they were irresistible to her. We had laughed together. So alike, the two of us. That was in the summer.

I went into the parlor and found Jeremiah's journal on the table by the yellow chair. From the number of pages written it was clear that he had been writing most of his waking hours during the visit—fifty close-written pages beginning with the plagiarism "Of The Farm."

With magnifying glass because of the smallness of the hand I read me, us. I read that Paul and I were lovers. I read that Jeremiah had observed us together during the Christmas visit. Jeremiah did not like to be disappointed; like all poets, he created his own world as he wished it to be, arranged and rearranged it for the effect wanted at the moment. Casual words, imaginary or not (some rang familiarly) were placed in contexts so alien to the characters of Paul and me that in comparison Beatrix's distortions were as the prattlings of children who light briefly upon grotesquerie through bouyancy, like butterflies. A number of times Paul and I, halves of one narcissist, as it were, were pushed, peas in gelatin, into the framework of *Tamburlaine*, itself a good model of poetically reordered history. It was evident that Jeremiah was at work on a highly personal approach to dramatic/poetic explication, using friends as his medium.

There were diversions: graphs as classic-appearing as diagrams of chess moves—Jeremiah recording successful facial expression as used at strategic times by himself during our holiday. In the summer he had looked at women newly met with subtle ruefulness which said "If only (we were alone; were not married; were married to each other)"; it was a very effective look, more so when one knew that it had been rehearsed with Jamesian calculation. On graph paper; might a mirror have failed to reflect anything at all?

Finally it was what Jeremiah did on paper to Beatrix that I found most affecting. We all write about loved ones, friends, acquaintances, sometimes even with insight, sometimes even kindly. But there was no emotion, not even spleen, in Jeremiah's clinic; only the eye of a computer, among the chimeras of our modern world, could be so pitiless.

They were still awake, lying propped on cushions reading. Their bodies were close together, one stem under the covers, with their heads leaning away toward separate lights. They were a rich sight, dark and burnished blooms on a slender stem. I was humbled by their beauty, by a trembling-kneed desire to be rid of it. My age bothered me unbeautifully at all joinings, humbling me further with faulty articulation.

I handed Jeremiah his journal and saw that the kindliest poet was waiting for a sign that I had read it. Of course I had been meant to. A man who plans his facial expressions does not forget his journal.

I told them about death. A plastic envelope of paranoia formed about Beatrix's head. I told them "I know you'll want to be there." I mentioned the early train. I mentioned packing tonight. The room, I let them see me seeing, badly needed cleaning and airing; price tags littered the floor; they must have bought all new clothes for Christmas.

Beatrix, softened for scarring, made me sorry. I thought that her abrasiveness and aggression could be meant to balance Jeremiah's secrecy: they were two wounds balancing each other. I imagined that she read his journal, each new installment soon as written. Reading herself would be like watching herself decay, seeing the pattern of her life and the end of her life as projected by God. Then I was less sorry for her: she had read herself in our journals, but where were we? What reality did we have, in some secret place of hers, that we did not know about? Her mimicry was awfully creative at times; what would the frozen static words do to us? Might she have crippled me, left off one of my limbs, lobotomized my memory, turned me for all eternity into an *unliberated woman*? As though she were reading my mind, she scratched her head: Beatrix in the zoo.

I have decided that I do not fancy myself as Jeremiah wrote me, in the guise of half-Tamburlaine. I will be whole or nothing. We shepherds, when the world comes to us, can grow ambitious and ambition can make us revert, forgetful of learned consequences. I was a stalker of quarry long before I wrote; in the South it is honorable to teach a child how to hunt; from the hunted he draws conclusions about survival.

I took the Dresdens to the ferry, but Miss Gold and I did not share the wait with them. I told them "At least you won't miss the boat." Beatrix's eyes were not too sure. Jeremiah briefly turned my meaning over and then withdrew into his famous decency.

Their bedroom was a shambles. Books had been pulled onto the floor—Beatrix might have written "as though in a search for meaning." I don't know how she might have written about the curiously old-fashioned device, obviously used, left in plain sight; perhaps a discourse on the right of women to frustrations quite apart from men and their biological cofunctioning or failure. The floor was still strewn with price tags. I fancied that they were a Brooklyn version of manners: Beatrix's way of indicating that they had quietly shared the price of our Christmas together.

THE TAUTOPHONE

ALFREDO GIULIANI

Translated by Luigi Ballerini

The tautophone is a psychological test, the auditory equivalent of Rorschach's inkblots: the patient is asked to listen to a record playing what would appear to be sentences, sounds that resemble sequences of words, but do not carry any specific semantic load. Just as the blot is indifferent in the face of interpretation (it could be a bat or, let us say, a vulva) so the unintelligible sentence is not to be identified with this or that meaning: we are persuaded to assign one to it, but they are all both "good" and pathological in various degrees. Interpreting the oracle we decode ourselves: the tautophone is the noise our music makes.

LETTER FROM THE MOUNTAIN THERAPY

dear father I slept like a lion then when the innocent
        sun inspected me
in a flash you were right suddenly all alone I crowded
        myself with nose and
my arms shoveling behind the panes I'd like to shatter
        the sparkling corpses
for smoke puffs cause the sun to turn and I've decided
        to let my mustache grow

it brings out the profile of my athletic jawbone
>and is very
useful to essence hunters since the children can
>mock me while I
cross the hotel lobby moving away down blind expanses
>finally
deserted by those monstrous screaming embryos with tails and
>peaks of vigor

my inner stingings I must act with calm lay them down upon
>the hairtips' sky
make them drip from eyelids' foam it is too dangerous
>hollows fade one
by one and all the ways out the heart can't be the heart
>does not ache trickles
annoyed would be a more fitting thing to say than fierce
>I'm very kind to everyone

to hide my independence even my Marienbad cousin
>is here and her pointed
knees I could use them she who thinks I am dismayed by her
>contemptuous immodesty
at the White Stag during an outing in '61 a real
>grackle with her falsetto
like a spoon stirred in a glass of water but at least
>we have earplugs

so damp they are or dry the tips deceive the thin layer of air
>electrified
by the impalpable and bored stroking of the symbols and of the
>space of three square
holes ridiculously lifted in the frightened void of windows
>and coal the air
is full of crosses that dig the snow and I already feel at night
>their bristly trotting

I MYSELF AND THE THEATER

in these long stretches of silence I lie under the vast
    skies of a service
stairway or else I perch thinking that those brave knights
    rode
their lurid wolf to dancing school it always turned out well for me
    when trying to understand
what I am thinking to interlock my fingers and extend thumbs
    and elbows

in the end she unfolds her rabbit cloak on hairy grass
    like you how sweet
the pelvic throb when she lifts up her knee and uncovers
    the snail the body is all
life size advancing like a dream the movements slackened
    in the plasma
I do not close my eyes my arms stretched out to drive
    upon a blazing truck

the tuna looks up through borders of scarlet sage it is blue-
    green like Chinese
turnips and there must be a secret meaning if the floor
    is of black glass
and tapered girls in unknown cities move ahead groping their
    way raising
big bubbles of tender perfume from under the moonbeams and
    also stumble

some of them dance on the glassy surface of a stream
    I see the delicate
lacework of the feet the forest is panting and an uncomprehending
    army of muscles transports
useful umbrellas on its back until a bunch of fleeing
    runaways pretends
to unload the diurnal tension into wolves' howls and
    they are the inhabitants

if I now seek to comprehend the neatness of the disconcerting
    waves of the tiger's

immobile body stunned or killed among the reeds I don't
     allow the third eye
to excite my forehead my anus would regret it to such a degree
     that I believe the theater
a work of mystery and applause supposed by intelligent men
     and beasts will revive

FABLE OF INDIGESTION

my mouth was watery my stomach completely botanic I put my
     liquid finger to the sugar bowl
looking at the black discarded suit hanging in that fetal time
     when they tied my ankles
it will be good for me I'd ponder astonished at the great
     production of thoughts to be almost dead
I caught one by the slippery neck and spat out the purulent
     words with pulp and pit

white ruffled larvae gush out sense of symbolic confidence
     that I am about to grunt
in dream the water opens end of the bubbles buttoning up of
     overcoat a shower of caps
squeaks of shoes shiny with cold and smoking hands of wool that
     thump courtyard lit
by a large electrical snail sly to the feathery swirls
     troops of bowings offal and wigs

periwinkles flashing from sullen throats of mushy venuses this
     is the confused moment to turn
aside abjection careful to cough up on sawdust it is a sign of
     grace oh dark dislocation
of chance a whiff from aphrodisiac stables distracts me
     "Lucullus" my aunt would exhilarate from the oven
totem and gas the thirteenth month the blood the rabbit digs
     the house quartan of explosion the cream

first a goodnatured batrachian sobs then a languid
    little fish joggles the
servant's tail then almost overcome by sleep the mute duck
    grumbles under the testicles
for me worshipper of mares the hippomaniac rustled as he ran
    delighting me a cry small eyes in the dark
waxed with lunar films tormented I was chasing the enormous
    inquisition of animal names

was fondling slow grim crowds and tribades like cows was stalking
    through limbos I swept by winds of insult
devouring fingers in my starch-soiled collar ah all the names
    were useless was laughing hard funny
& mystic and this dollydoll is the cramp of the crocodile bird
    and the autumn of the bat the ecstasy
of the silent pap-gnat the longed for spirit that you have to return
    to this night that only digested the rabbit

ONAN'S CANDLE

I want to stay like this hunched up my feet are very
    long my claws also claim
a good-night kiss reminds me of how keen I was on wearing
    a hat well low on my head
so I could take it off and look at them from space although
    a weakened and burning novice
intruder in wet rays imprinted on the strawstack invisible ahah
    and let them be back there

blister's eye among cicada walls I feel my underpants slip off
    I clutch the blown-out candle
convulsively revolving in the wind around the strawstack I
    am alone against all the dark sides
with me sadness is when a man passes behind his face takes flight
    to the ground leaf that
should not want I pause in the shrill thicket I'm bored because
    the road must turn back under

nomadic fingers gunned down birds that is now full of quilts
    I shiver in the heart's descent
to the throat I bump against the tub of turds touched by the sky
    after all so in tenderness I piss
I place a pause into the fury they let loose they all have gone
    the countryside is bald and putrid
perhaps they walk the waterfall laughing they fluff me
    the bed crumbles to the skin

while the watchmaker sleeps with an eye on the sinkdrain
    finally each hair recedes
to its warm cell the tailor's wife stands her mouth agape
    on the white tiles
of the public john a decal of sleep is set in Onan's marrow
    oh quick quick ooh
"let me tell you the terrible thing" and they beautiful rustling
    calculating rabbits the lust

blind nonchalant actress slobber crowd spat by a bird they
    swallow bladefuls of cells
appetizing turds glitter under fresh laundry glup glup
    osh osh pantheism screwed
I strawstack dog rooster of resurrection here in my pierced
    sky shouting kok kuk kak
there's still some peel left devil's shit cover me to the eyes
    stench of plucked chicken

FOUR POEMS

CLAUDIO RODRIGUEZ

Translated by Louis M. Bourne

WITCHES AT NOON

(Toward knowledge)

I
They do not belong to old women
Nor to needles without eyes nor to pins
Without heads. This simple sorcery,
This old enchantment,
Doesn't skip like salt
In the fire. Neither a holy water
Sprinkler nor a virgin wax
Candle is needed. Each form
Of life has
A boiling point, a meteor
Of bubbles. There, where the lottery
Of the senses seeks
Its nature, there, where
Being congeals, in that
Living fibre, the witchcraft
Dwells. It's not only the body,
With its legend of dullness,

110

That deceives us: in the very
Make-up of matter, in such
Clarity which is a trick,
Winks, potions, disquieting
Carmen, upset us. And this
September noon smells of a black
And oily hood, of pure witch;
And in the folds of air,
On the altars of space, there are
Buried vices, places
Where the heart is bought, sinister
Recipes for love. And in the taut
Ripeness of the day, not a pair of lips
But dry gums
Suck prayer and blasphemy,
Memory and forgetfulness,
From our blood,
All that was calm or feverish.
Like one who reads a life's
Repentance in a crossed-out line,
With firmness, with piety, faith, even with hate,
Now at noon, when it's
Hot and the taste is
Deadened, we contemplate
The deep ravage and stubborn progress
Of things, their endless
Delirium, while the swallows
Squeal in flight.

II
Mountain flowers, stale lard,
A child's navel, verbena
From the morning of Saint John's Day,
The armless puppet, resin
Good for a woman's hips,
Saffron, the short thistle, the stewpot
From Talavera with pepper and wine,
Everything that belongs to witches,
Natural things, today are nothing

Compared to this witches' sabbath
Of images which, now,
When beings leave hardly any shadow,
Produces a reflection: life.
Life is not a reflection,
But what is its image?
Does one body on another
Feel resurrection or death? How can
We poison and purify
This air which is no lung of ours?
Why does the lover never
Seek truth, but happiness instead?
How can happiness exist
Without truth? Here's the rub.

But we never
Touch the suture,
That seam (sometimes patchwork,
Sometimes embroidery),
Between our senses and outward things,
That fine sand
Which smells not sweet now but salty,
Where the river and the sea combine,
One echo in another, the fragments
Of a dream for which I gave a world
And will continue giving. Among the ruins
Of the sun, a nest
Trembles with nocturnal heat. Among
Our laws' disgrace, arises
The altarpiece with old
Gold and the old doctrine
Of new justice. In what markets
Of great pilfering is the water
Wine, the wine blood, the blood thirst?
Through which customs
Is flour smuggled in
As flesh, the flesh
As dust and the dust
As future flesh?

This is a matter for fools. A common
Crime is this walking among the pinches
Of witches. For they don't
Study but dance
And piss and are the friends
Of taverns. And now,
At noon,
If they kiss us from so many things,
Where will their night be found,
Where their lips, where our mouth
To accept so many lies and so much
Love?

SPARROW

He doesn't forget. This
Crafty urchin doesn't
Leave our life. Always
Hard up, nowhere to go,
He walks here like anyone,
Stubbornly bathes here
Among our shoes.
What does he seek in our dark
Life? What love does he find
In our bread so hard? He already
Left the air to the dying,
This sparrow, who could have
Flown off, but here he stays,
Here below, secure,
Stuffing all the dust
Of the world in his breast.

MONEY

Shall I sell my words, today when I lack
Value, income, today when none will give me credit?
I need money for love, poverty
For loving. And the price of a memory, the auctioning
Of a vice, the inventory of a desire,
Give value, not virtue, to my needs,
A wide vocabulary to my debasements,
License to my caustic
Loneliness. Because money is sometimes a dream
Itself, the very quality
Of life. And its triumph, its monopoly, gives fervency,
Change, imagination, removes old age and clears away
Frowning, and increases friends
And raises skirts, and is honey
Crystallizing light, heat. No plague, leprosy
Like today; merriment,
Not frivolity; law,
Not impunity. Shall I sell these words
Then? I, rich from so much loss,
Without stratagems, penniless, even untempted
And free from gilded ruin? What is the burrow
Of these words for which, though giving spirit,
Earn no money? Do they insure bread or arms?
Or rather, as a poorly contrived balance sheet,
Do they try to order a time of want,
To give meaning to a life: ownership or eviction?

FOAM

I am watching the foam, its delicateness
Which is so different from that of ash.
Like a man who beholds a smile, the one
For which he gives his life and it is anxiety
And shelter for him, now I watch the humble
Foam. It is the beautiful, rough moment

Of use, the friction, the act of offerance
Creating it. The imprisoned pain
Of the sea is overcome in so light a fibre.
Beneath the keel, facing the embankment, where
Furrowed love exists, the foam is born
Like the flower on earth. And it is in it
That death breaks, in its skein
That the sea takes life, as man is man
At the peak of his passion, apart
From other concerns: in his living sperm.
At this railing, curbstone of matter,
Which is a spring, not an outlet,
I lean forward now, when the tide
Rises, and there I sink, there I drown
So silently, with complete
Acceptance, uninjured, renewed
In the imperishable foam.

GORBY AND THE RATS

OMAR POUND

Adapted from the Persian of Obeyd-i-Zakani

*Obeyd-i-Zakani was born in Qazvin in northern Persia about A.D.
1300 of a distinguished local family. He spent at least twelve years
in Shiraz as a learned man, where he wrote a treatise on Arabic
grammar. Eventually he returned to Qazvin, became a local judge,
and tutored sons of the provincial nobility. He died in 1371.*

*Throughout his life Obeyd wrote much scurrilous but comic sa-
tire, in prose and verse. Living during the Mongol occupation
which began in 1220, he saw his country devastated politically and
economically, particularly after 1335, with the Mongol central
government weakened, and usurping princes taxing ungrown crops,
livestock, anything tangible, whenever and wherever they could—
the naïve peasants suffering the most.*

Gorby and the Rats ("Mush-o-gurbeh") *is political satire, the
cats are probably rapacious local Mongol princes and the rats na-
tive Persian peasants. The poem also parodies classical Persian epic
and lyrical poetry, and makes constant fun of the subtly graded
honorifics of Persian culture and the instinctive dissembling neces-
sary in a country so often overrun by foreign invaders. Persian
children still read this tale. The author's moral, if any, appears to
be that cats do not change their nature. To forgive is human—to
purr, feline.*

Long long ago
when God was, for without Him nothing was,
and Time had just begun
Heaven decreed a cat should dwell
in a city called Kirmàn.

The cat was Gorby
and his reputation caused great alarm
throughout the land of Persia.
His tail was borrowed from a lion
his paws were golden eagle's claws
his chest a silver shield
and every whisker was a sword.

Once, it is said, four lions
dining on honest prey
hearing this dragon-cat roar seven miles away
left their feast unfinished
and with prudence and in peace
slunk
silently
away.

In fact
he was no purring pusillanimous puss.
HE was a CAT, whose paws were the law
and THAT was THAT

When Gorby was hungry he used to hide
in a cellar the rats monopolised,
and like a robber in a park
he'd crouch behind full jars of wine
and inside vats
waiting to pounce on well-wined rats.

One day
a noisy rat jumped from the cellar wall
dipped his nose and drank,
and drank
and drank his fill
until he thought his squeak a lion's roar.

"Where's that cataleptic kit,
that feline fraud," he growled,
"I'll knot his whiskers, nip his neck
and stuff his hide with straw,
or is pretty little fluffkin scaredy-cat
afraid to meet on the open battle-floor?"

Gorby, still silent, yawned and filed his claws.

Suddenly he pounced, like a tiger on a mountain goat
"You're doomed," he miaowed, and grabbed the drunkard's
throat.

The rat, his larynx almost severed, whispered, "Gorby dear
your eyes are lanterns leading us to Paradise. Your fur . . .
Forgive me, I have dined too well for humble folk.
Sweet wine has soured my words and fouled my soul
but I am innocent. It was the wine that spoke."

"Rats," said Gorby, "your tongue has never tasted truth,
and I am deaf to lies.
I heard you call me 'Ali-cat,' and worse,
you paper-rat, all filth and fleas,
muscleman indeed! I'll Mussulman you!
I'll weary your wife with waiting,
she'll need another mate now."

In short, cat ate rat, then,
conforming to the ritual laws
washed his whiskers, face, and claws,
and with all humility
went to the mosque and prayed:

Creator of the Universe,
this cat repents with contrite heart
the Muslim blood he used to shed
in rats he tore apart.
Be Clement, be Merciful,
I'll wrong them no more
and here renounce all ratting
and promise alms to the poor.

By Heaven's whim
a hidden mosque-rat overheard
puss's promised virtue to his Lord
and before the cat could change his mind
the rat had bustled off to spread the news
to all ratkind.

"Gorby has repented. Gorby has repented.
I saw him in the mosque today
like a pious mullah, beads in paw,
wailing and praying
eyes cast down towards the floor.
O Allah is Compassionate and Merciful is His Name,
dear puss is one of us again."

They pranced and danced and sang,
"dear puss is one of us again,"
and drank and drank,
". . . is pussulman again."

Then up stepped The Seven
the noblest of them all, and said,
"Our love for puss is such
we nominate each other
to carry a feast to his celestial hall."

One brought wine,
the next: a whole roast lamb,
another: sweet raisins from his estate
the fourth, seven dates as big as mice
the fifth, a bag of fragrant cheese
which was to have been his New Year's feast.
Another thought yoghurt would bring peace
to his digestion,
and the seventh, proudest of them all,
carried above his turbaned brow
a bowl of great price, heaped with pilàw
nightingales' wings
almonds and rice
decked with sweet lemon rind and spice;

and murmuring salaams in puss's praise
they marched to the palace
for audience with the cat.

There they were hastily ushered in.
They bowed, fell reverently upon their paws
and squeaked:
"Our heads are gravel beneath your silken paws
our souls but footstools at your feet
taste these slight refreshments, accept our humble pie,
so we may praise your goodness
and serve you till we die."

"Tis true," the cat replied, "our Holy Book doth say,
'Heaven rewards the pious and the faithful,' and I,
as only Allah knows, have fasted long enough to please Him,
for Behold!—my Reward!
Here you are—a portion
of the Bounty I am worthy of . . .
but pardon me,
wondering how to serve you best
I quite forgot myself.
Your presence is my soul's true nourishment.
Come near my dears and sit by me.
O Allah! What fools these morsels be!
Come closer, beside me, on this sofa.
Near's too far—I wish you were all inside me."

The rats advanced, each a quivering willow branch.
"Now," said Gorby, "let us prey,"
and springing like a lion, grabbed the nearest five
two per paw, while one
hung loosely from his jaw—alive.

Tailless but with a tale to tell
the two survivors fled.
"That cat," they said, "has slain
five princes of our realm
and all you do is murmur:
'Peace be upon you, peace';

FIVE, belovèd of our clan
torn apart while still alive,
may death be their release
and SHAME, everlasting shame—YOUR only glory."

And dusting themselves with sands of woe
they blacked their brows
dipped their tails in sorrow's mead, and howled,
"To the Capitol, and there we'll tell our King."

King Rat, aloof upon his throne
saw them coming from afar
and wondering what they wanted
ordered the palace gates slightly ajar.

The rats came in, bowed in unison and sang:

O Royal Rodent, King of Kings
for whom all rodents pray
five princeling rats, five rodent lives
were swallowed up today.

Rex rattus! Rex rattus!
Our humble hearts are sad,
O Monarch of all ages
that feline has gone mad.
He used to snatch but one a year
and now he swallows five
yet still proclaims his piety
to those he's left alive.

The Royal Anger rose
and clothed its words in pride.
(Here's vengeance for your storybooks)
"THAT CAT MUST DIE!
or thirty thousand Mussulmèn
shall know the reason why."

Within a week the Palace Guard
armed with lances, arrows, slings and swords

were joined by loyal peasant hordes
from Khurasàn and Resht;
pack rats with catgut for catapults and kitbags for cats
rattletrap and samovars, and poisoned snacks.

The army ready, "Wisdom of the Ages,"
an elder in the Royal Ratinue
squeaked sagely,
"We must despatch a diplomat
with a knack for rhatoric to tell that cat
IT'S WAR OR SUBMISSION"
and soon
an envoy had scurried to Gorby Hall
to gently breathe his mission.

"His Majesty orders his humble envoy, me,
to beg your presence at his court, professing loyalty,
and bids me to inform you
his army numbers thousands, whose loyalty is sure;
Alas! O lustrous furry one,
IT'S FEALTY or WAR."

"Cat-fodder," snarled Gorby, "go away.
I am in command here, and in Kirmàn I stay,"
and secretly mustered an army of cats,
regiments from Isfahan and Princes from Yazd.

By the great salt desert marched the rats
across mountain passes rode the cats
to the open Plain of Fàrs,
and there both armies met and fought
paw to paw in battle, like heroes from the past.

In every corner of the field unnumbered lie the dead,
as vanguards fall, reserves stand still—
no space for lances, horse or shield,
and nowhere else to tread.

Then right to the centre the Feline Guard attacks
as a regiment of rodents turns tail in its tracks,

confusion and chaos   havoc and doubt
as cat after cat wins every bout
and many a rat is routed.

Then suddenly arose   a cry of valour
"The cat is down,"   All Praise to Allah.
"Rally, rats! Rally!"

There lay Gorby groaning on the ground
his stallion's heel nipped by a rat
who swore to bring him down.
Puss to dust. Alas!
There Gorby lay
groaning several lives away
on the Plain of Fàrs.

"Catch him! Bind him! Truss him up!"
squeaked seven rat-lion-cubs,
"tie his paws with string,
tie 'em tight and mind his claws,
then WE
will take him to our King."
(Loud applause.)

They danced and pranced and beat the drum of joy
until they reached the court.

And there, King Rat, seeing the cat was safely tied
scowled and shouted:
"Foul inhuman beast! You lied!
You ate my army, you greedy thing,
and worse—without the Royal Permission."
"Alas," sighed Gorby,
"my face is black with shame and sin,
my soulless soul now pleads and craves
your Royal Renown for Clemency
to save my worthless skin.
Hear my purr for pardon, Lord,
Hear my purrrrrrrrrr."
His words were wet with weeping.

"To the gibbet with that dog of a cat,"
the King shouted.
"In recompense for all the noble necks he broke
I myself will ride the Royal Elephant
to watch him swing
and die."

And surrounded by his army
fore and aft
he rode in triumph through the town
to hear the music of his citizens
who cheered and laughed.
And there in the market place tied to the gallows
stood Gorby, miaowing and caterwauling sorrows.

"What! Do I hear a miaow from that black Kirmàni cow?
Is he still alive, when I decreed THAT CAT MUST DIE,
AND NOW."

Some edged back by nudging others on
their chatter soon became a murmur,
till all had swallowed silence and were dumb.
Not a rat stirred.
Not a rat in all the rout
dared step up and hang the cat,
not to win all Persia.

The King, sorrowed by their shame
and furious at their fear
quivered angrily,
"What! Are we starved of heroes here?
You rattle-tattle rodent bipeds,
you slinking sewer rats.
May every feline in Kirmàn
feast off you tonight."
And stepping forward, single-pawed
he raised his sword
to cut the cat in two.

When Gorby saw the King of Rats
he suddenly became a dragoned-lion again,

his courage boiled, the cauldron of his fury spilled,
he tore his cords asunder,
spread his golden eagle's claws
unsheathed each whiskered quill and sword
and levelled every rat
so none would rise again—
except as dust.

Which ends my tale. The army fled.
King Rat deserted.
Howdah and kingdom tumbled down,
while I,
steeped in the wine of wonder
asked the meaning of this yarn.
"The meaning's clear," the poet said,
"if you are wise enough to see it.
It is . . ."   But then, alas,
came the allotted span,
Allah called,
our poet heard his name:

OBEYD

and passed away.

*. . . and as in every chestnut lies
Truth's Kernel—so in every tale.*

THE WINDOW

YANNIS RITSOS

Translated by Rae Dalven

*Two men are seated near the window of a room by the sea. They
appear to be old friends who have not met for a long time. One of
them looks like a seaman. The other—the one who is speaking—is
not. Night is falling slowly—it is a calm spring evening, violet-
colored and purple. The sea opposite, smooth as oil, illumines with
undulating streaked reflections, the ship's sides, the ropes, the
masts, the houses. Simply and somewhat wearily at the start:*

I sit here by the window; I gaze at the passers-by
and I see myself in their eyes. I think that I am
a silent photograph, in its old picture frame,
hanging outside the house, on the west wall,
me and my window.
                    Sometimes I myself look at
this photograph with its amorous, weary eyes—
a shadow conceals the mouth; at moments the surface glint of
      the glass
in the picture frame, facing the setting sun or the moonlight,
covers the face completely and I am concealed
behind a square-shaped light, pale, or silvery or rosy,
and I can look at the world in freedom
without anyone seeing me. In freedom; what can one say?

I cannot move; against my back
is the damp or burning wall; against my chest
the cold windowpane; the tiny veins of my eyes
are branched out on the windowpane. And so, pressed
between the wall and the windowpane, I do not dare move
        my hand,
bring the palm of my hand up to my eyebrows when the
        sun sparkles
like an implacable glory; and I am obliged
to see and desire and not be able to move. If I try
to touch something, my elbow could
break the windowpane, and leave
a hole on my side,—exposed to the rain and the glances.
Then again if I try to speak, the breath of my voice
clouds up the windowpane (as it does now),
and I can no longer see the thing I should like to talk about.

.   .   .

Silence and immobility then. You can even call it hypocrisy
because you know, perhaps, how many crucified clamors,
how many genuflecting gestures dwell
behind the vertical crystalline splendor.
Especially when evening falls, now in the spring, and the harbor
is a faraway fire, golden and red,
inside the darkened forest of masts, and you sense
the fish, compressed by the water, rising
to the surface with their mouths open like little triangles
to inhale a very deep breath;—have you noticed?
at such times the dense light of the water is fractured
by thousands of open mouths of little fish. No one can endure
indefinitely under the mass of water, in these mythical
        marine forests,
in that asphyxiating transparency with this boundless
        perilous view.

.   .   .

I think that in the same way, the photographs also cannot endure
        behind their picture glass

no matter what the pose, however lovely, no matter what the
    moment in their lives
in a time-stopped age, in an hour of prideful purity,
with their exquisite, youthful hands resting on the elegant
    table of the photograph studio,
or on their knees with an unfading flower (naturally) in
    their lapel,
with a hardly perceptible, triumphant smile on their lips,
not too broad, so as to betray haughtiness,
nor yet again completely constrained, so as to betray submission
    to destiny.
But time lies totally in ambush, before and beyond their
    beautiful moment,
and they desire their time intact, even if they should lose
this fossilized dignity of theirs, this
splendid pose of theirs, premeditated or no—indifferently,
even if their upright legend should melt like a white candle
    beneath the flame of their eyes,
even if their youthfulness coming out of the light of the crystal
    should be belied.

.   .   .

But then again, fear appears larger than their desire
or perhaps it is equal to it; and then their smile
is also like a silvery fish, elongated and stopped
between two boulders of the deep—or it is like
an ash-colored bird with motionless wings, balanced in the air,
immobile within its own motion. And the photographs remain
locked in there, with all their repentance or their remorse, and
    even their hostility,
without coming out of their picture frame, out of their desire
    and their fear,
facing the importunate sky and the measureless sea.

.   .   .

This is why we often select a narrow space to protect us
from our own immensity. And perhaps this is why
I sit here, at this window, to gaze at

the fresh tracks of the bare feet of the boatman,
on the flagstones of the quay, erasing little by little,
like a row of little oblong moons inside a fairy tale.

         •   •   •

And I cannot understand anything any longer, nor do I try
    to understand.
A woman with her hair washed leans over to the adjacent balcony,
    singing softly
to dry her hair with her song. A sailor
stands astonished, with legs spread apart,
before his enormous afternoon shadow, as if he is
standing erect at the prow of a ship, in a foreign port,
and he does not know the waters, and he does not know where
    to cast anchor.
Later, as it slowly darkens, and the silent, violet
palpitation of the setting sun fades on the walls and the
    enclosure, even before
the street lanterns are lighted, a sudden heat comes on—and then
the faces are more often guessed at than that they are;
you see the shadow penetrating into the perspiring armpits;
the sound of a fleeting dress fans the foliage of a tree;
the white shirts of the youth take on a faraway azure color
    and they give off vapor,
and everything is so isolated, bewitched and uncaught, that
perhaps this is why
all the lights go on at once, certain to dissolve all in
    their precision.

         •   •   •

Inside the houses, the sheets resemble drooping flags
in an inexplicable ocean calmness, when all have left the ship
and the flags have no one for whom to unfurl and they hang limp
    in the evening
heated by the sun, forgotten, languid
like flayed hides of huge animals they slaughtered
on a day of public celebration, with parades, music, dances
    and banquets.

The celebration is over. The streets are deserted.
      On the sidewalks
are oily papers, trampled cockades, pieces of crust, bones—
and yet, no one has returned to his home, as if he had repented,
as if all had taken an extension they did not need.

        ·   ·   ·

The rooms remain dark and unappetizing, lighted only
by the multicolored street lights and the ships or by a few
      distracted stars,
or by the sudden searchlight of a cargo boat passing by loaded
with drunken infantrymen, shouts and songs,
and the searchlight nails the shadow of the window inside
      the house
mutely and discreetly as if it were a large wooden crate
that two obscure-looking sailors carry over to a deserted shore.

        ·   ·   ·

Then some peculiar ideas come to you,—doesn't this happen to
      you too?
As if each one of us is two persons
with covered faces, and the two of them rancorous,
unable to understand each other, and only at this very moment
      have they agreed
to carry this large crate, to dig with their nails
a little beyond the shore, to bury it.

        ·   ·   ·

And you know it too, just as they do, despite all their secrecy,
that inside this large crate lies a mutilated body,
a youthful, dearly beloved body; and the single
body is theirs, that they themselves murdered, and they
      buried it,
as if they were two strangers.
                      This large crate
with the impeccable shape, a regular square,
resembles a closed door,

resembles those photographs in their picture frames that we were
     talking about,
resembles this window from where we look at the lovely movement
     on the street in the spring.

.   .   .

Often, I have encountered this body, this face,
especially on moonlight nights, strolling
—somewhat pale,—but always youthful—on the quay
or on the street above the dirty brothels,
with the painted women, the hungry dogs, the rusty sheet-irons,
with the unshaven sailors, the rotten fruit, the blasphemies,
     the empty-halves of squeezed lemons,
the green washrooms, the basins, the spermaceti, the acetylenes.
Indeed, sometimes I have seen him bargaining with a woman,
but she would not accept because he was offering her too much.
     "No, no," she kept on saying.
"It cannot be done. No," with a hoarse voice, and her hand
with the red fingernails, trembled a little. She was afraid
they might even involve her in some thefts, embezzlements,
     passkeys,
with huge iron gates like those the fortunetellers
     always predict
and in truth, that are never lacking. Why did she need
     these things?
The price was fixed,—not, of course, any less but not
     any more either.

.   .   .

An incomprehensible person, with eyes that were
enormous and uninhabited on his pale face,
like live coals. They could even scorch her.
They could even melt her hairpins
and the melted burning iron could run down the furrows of her
     hair, into her eyes.
He always looked sad—perhaps because of his strength
that he had never managed to kill;—a beautiful sorrow
like the wide afternoon melancholy of spring. And it became him,

and was almost necessary to him. He had never been
mutilated, as we believe. He would open that large crate calmly,
as if he were opening a door, and he would come out intact under
    the moon,
and his veins would be traced intensely in his hands,
red, so red—curious, in such a moonlight,
beneath his pale Christian skin.

                    •   •   •

Honestly, sometimes I think that mutilation
can keep us whole, provided we know it,
and how can we not know it since it is our knowledge
that mutilates us and puts us together again with those things
    we denied.

                    •   •   •

On the street above, I was telling you about, there are pretty—
the most unlikely shops in the world—second-hand shops, coal
        stores, grocery stores,
barbershops with old lithographs and heavy
        conspiratorial armchairs,
butcher shops with large mirrors that reflect a multiplication
of slaughtered lambs and beef in a red procession;
fruit and vegetable stores and fishmarkets, the odors of the fish
        commingling with the fruit—
a suspicious, taciturn clamor in front of the doorways,
a mute illumination like a reflection of leaves of white iron
or of large yellow planed boards,
leaning upright against the front of the carpentry shop.
        Up there they are selling pell-mell,
raincoats, poultry, clothespins, bottles, combs,
biscuits in iron boxes, cheap coffins, perfumed soap,
rusty cabins from shipwrecked boats they had brought out to be
        sold at auction,
and later they pulled out piece by piece,
silks from various lands with all sorts of designs and colors,
        not cleared by customs,
Japanese tea services, hashish and tablecloths,

and some odd-looking cages vaulted like half-completed churches,
inside which some unfamiliar rose-golden birds watch
the movement on the street with two strange impenetrable eyes
like two yellow and black pebbles, stolen in the night from the
    fingers of the dead.

．　　．　　．

Barefoot children shoot crap in the middle of the road,
women sleep with sailors in low-ceilinged rooms with
    open windows,
sun-tanned itinerant little merchants piss in a line in
    the enclosure;
from time to time, the fish glisten in the baskets like enormous
    bloodstained knives
and sometimes, a bee gone astray
wanders around over there, perplexed, buzzing,
and leaving in the air the golden, wire spirals of her whirlings,
like little springs from some childish, dissembowelled toy.

．　　．　　．

A cloud of dust moves slowly at twilight among the faces,
like a cherry-colored secret of inhalations, perspirations,
    self-interests and crimes,
a deep secret of an inexhaustible hunger hastily nurtured
an interminable coming and going, an interminable bargaining,
    an interminable expenditure
in support of commerce, ambitions, the shrewdly clever, and life,
    naturally.
Sometimes you see a lovely young girl wearing a clean,
    flowery dress,
standing on the soot-filled street, beside the little pistachio
    cart and the sacks,
entirely illumined by the sea
and smiling with two rows of virgin teeth, toward the whistle
    of a ship.

．　　．　　．

Around her, the rotted empty halves of squeezed lemons shine
    like small suns;
a little calico curtain, pulled back aslant at a low window,
is like a dog-eared page of a beloved book
to remind you to return at some future time to reread it.

            •   •   •

So there is no humiliation where life wants to live,
where dogs search the rubbish heap with noble movements
and young girls hold high their unlined foreheads loaded with
    their robust hair,
as if they are carrying a black pitcher of silent water,
in fear lest they drop it. I have seen many young girls
in this posture, yes, on that very street,
and dark-complected, hairy young men with fleshy mouths,
always in anger (the way the very sad are)
who did not manage to become as vulgar as they should
    have liked
and this is why they blaspheme always more and more, in a voice
    always heavier. If you observe carefully
you will understand. Their voice is
a wide palm of the hand caressing the black cat of the ship
seated sagely on their knees—at nighttime naturally,
and neither their hand, nor the cat is visible. Only the cat's
    eyes phosphoresce
like two flanking lights on a rowboat coasting along a
    flowery isle.

            •   •   •

If you go up that street a little further, to the hillock of
    Saint Basil,
you will see the whole harbor stretched out under your eyes,
you will see glittering on the darkened water, at the edge of
    the boundless sea,
the large gold-green irridescent stains of oil or petroleum,
brilliant stains, and immaculate you could say, like bright
    moving little isles of an indifferent calm
among dead dogs, rotten potatoes, straw, pine cones and rowboats.

            •   •   •

So you can watch unhesitating from this window
or you can even go out on the street. A silent sanctity
remains under the actions of people. A violet-colored shadow
is silent on the left shoulder of a woman wearied by love,
who turned over from her other side and sleeps alone.
       You can see
the heavy drawers hanging in the next courtyard, stained by
       nocturnal emissions
or the unfolded condoms underneath the park benches
or the buttons from the women's corsages that have fallen on
       the grass
like little mother-of-pearl flowers, slightly grieved
because they no longer have anything else to offer—perfume,
       pollen, seed. Nothing.

                    .   .   .

I myself once thought of going out on that street
to sell this window and that large crate
for no other reason than to relieve myself of their care,
so I too might get involved in buying and selling,
to listen to my voice when it speaks in a foreign tongue.
       I sensed very early
that I had nothing to sell. It was only an ulterior motive:
the probing for a new proof that again
I would have supervised from this window, even
       without windowpanes.

                    .   .   .

I have never succeeded in business. Besides, I do not have
anything worth paying for, nothing
that I can pay for. And these old photographs
are worth nothing to others, although their picture frames
       at least
are of solid gold. But to me they are necessary.

                    .   .   .

And neither are they dead—no. When evening falls
and the chairs outside the cafés are still warm
and everyone (and perhaps I too) demands to take
          refuge elsewhere,
they descend silently from their picture frame, as if they
          are descending
a lowly wooden staircase, they go into the kitchen,
they light the lamp, they set the table (you can hear
the friendly sound of a fork that has struck a plate),
they arrange my few books and even my thoughts
with comparisons and images (old and new), with
          modest arguments
and sometimes with ancient, unshakable, living proofs.

                    •   •   •

And this as well is why I hold on to this window, gratefully.
It does not hinder me from seeing and from being—quite
          the contrary.

                    •   •   •

As for the thing I was telling you about: "pressed between
          the wall and the windowpane,"
that was spring exaggeration, an exaggeration
of the carnal abundance of the foliage. The window
is a serviceable, square-shaped serenity and transparency.

                    •   •   •

When the walls cloud up in the twilight, this window
even lights up, as if by itself; it maintains and prolongs
the last reflection of the setting sun,
it casts its reflection on the shaded street,
it lights up the faces of the passers-by as if it catches
          them red-handed
in their most unfeigned moment; it lights up the wheels of
          the bicycles
or the gold chain plunged into the breast of a woman
or the strange name of a ship anchored in the harbor.

                    •   •   •

On these windowpanes, in the winter, the wind knocks his knees
and I see him departing in anger, facing about his
      broad shoulders.
Again, at other times, from here, on spring evenings, just as on
      this evening,
I listen to the conversations of sailors from one ship to
      the other,
as if they are revealing to me the rapport of the stars; as if
      they are explaining to me
those incomprehensible numbers on the ship's sides. All at once
I hear the noise of an anchor plunging into the water
like something being offered exclusively to me
like something authorizing me to point it out.

           •   •   •

Then what complaint can I have of this window?
If you wish you can open it halfway and, without looking outside
      at all,
through the windowpanes, you can follow unseen
authentic street scenes, in a space deeper and more enduring
with the soft illumination of the great distance,
although all these things are acted out right under your eyes,
      only a few steps away.
Then again if you wish you can open it all the way and look
      at yourself in the windowpane, as if inside
a distant magical mirror, and comb your hair that is
      thinning out,
or arrange your smile a little. Through these windowpanes
everything appears clearer—more silent, more unmoving,
consequently indispensable and ageless.
                    Did you ever happen to look
at the ocean through a water glass? Underneath the
      agitated surface
the bottom appears superb in its immobility
in a crystalline order, at once imperturbable and fragile,
in a mute sanctity—as we were saying. Only that
your breath is caught somewhat, if you remain like this for a
      longer time,
this is why you lift your head once more to the air,

or you open this window (now however knowing), or you go
    outside the door.

.   .   .

And there is no longer anything that can bend your life and
    your eyes,
and there is nothing that you cannot show proudly and sing it,
and there is nothing whose form you cannot turn toward the sun.

*They have shut the window and gone out on the street. The lights
of the ship were already lit. They reached the edge of the jetty.
They stopped, looked at the sea, heard the interrupted leap of a fish
in the shallow water, and, for no reason, they shook hands, palm to
palm. Then they sat silently on a coil of damp cable, they lit a
cigarette, and looked at themselves in the flame of the match. They
appeared strange and almost unjustifiably happy, with this inex-
plicable good fortune that life always has in the spring, when all
around the smell of the brine is mingled with the smell of fried
whitebait, cut lettuce and vinegar. In a little while they will go to
the tavern next door, to eat. They are already hungry. The sound of
the gramophone strengthened healthily this feeling of hunger. The
harbor sentry passed beside them, at their regular pace, and their
summer outfits whitened them in the evening. The two friends got
up from the cable and went on.*

Piraeus—April 1959

WHILE SUSAN HAYWARD WEEPS

FREDERICK BUSCH

Good Friday, and the sun has risen at 5:27, something new occurs in the year today, and he is here to witness. He has risen after slouching most of the night before his television set, the king before his fool, and his kidneys ache so dangerously, he feels he will break if he bends his back. So he moves in the vertical once he has opened the store—head back on his neck, neck unbending, spine uncurled. He walks like a man who carries a wholly filled cup of something hot. He goes slowly from the lightswitch past the sale table, past the undusted counter and through the uncurtained open door to his storeroom. At this lightswitch he is straight; when he moves his arm to move his hand to move the switch up, the rest of him stands still, and nothing spills.

All night the same commercial message was repeated on his blue set humming in the darkness, sound so low he hardly heard, and hardly cared to hear, sleeping and waking from commercial to commercial through the movies of the night. Myrna Loy was stilled for this and later, in another waking, Richard Egan with his glistery eyes, and then Susan Hayward, Victor Mature. And later, once again, there was Susan Hayward, little pouter pigeon of sadnesses, who held her pauses, or fell into silence, and who was followed by the gray-blue stare of the set and then by the high hard hum which meant that sound was coming and then by the blackness of the taped commercial and then by the music of momentousness and then the message itself: something about aspirin in which two hollow models of the human body, side by side, turned together as if they were dancers on a turning stage. The bodies had no heads. Their organs were transparent, and the powders of aspirin in a clear solution floated slowly in their plastic tracts. Each body wore a transparent loincloth, and behind the loincloth you could see they had no loins, nothing but clarity: you saw through the loincloth out their clear plastic buttocks and beyond, into the portentous black background that the commercial, like its aspirins, swam in until it dissolved—into Susan Hayward again, weeping for Victor Mature.

And this morning, as he hangs his brown imitation tweed-weave sportcoat on a red enameled hook, and as he opens his white plastic coffee cup and unwraps the Danish, as he hangs straight up and down on the hook of his pain, he sees the twin plastic bodies turning slowly into view from the background of their blackness, their absences hidden by earnest transparencies, turning into view as he turned out of sleep and then fell back again as they—headless statues in a garden of static and hums—fell back again to wait and then to once more slowly turn into view when Susan Hayward and Victor Mature fell from light.

As he winces in steam and, lips burned, chews the Danish with his lips slightly open, he looks at the two large steel-banded cartons of books to be opened, the eight or ten Jiffy bags, rubber-banded packet of invoices and, maybe, orders. The small Sears crowbar lies on the nearest carton of books, and he says "You'll have to climb up to me, 'cause I ain't bending nohow." Then he finishes the pastry, smacking his open lips as he chews, pulling with his mouth at the air above the coffee to suck some up without scalding himself. He crumples the plastic cup and sings "Ah ain't bendin' nohow" to his own invented tune and stands, his hands on his hips, looking at the tool he cannot reach.

All right, he will work standing up today. He will work at the counter in front, and at the telephone, and he will dust the shelves he can reach without stretching his back. Or he will not work at all, and close the store—hang out a card that says *Closed for Good Friday*—and then go home to lie on the floor until his back, that loosened part of him today that does not fit, will once more let him move like a man instead of a stalk, a praying mantis, something tall and in a carapace of pain.

"Ah ain't bendin' nohow" he sings. He nods his head and then says "But." He says "Nobody says you ain't lyin'." And he slowly lowers himself to a squat, his back unbent, and then drops his long fingers to the concrete floor, hesitates, puts more pressure on them, achingly thrusts a leg slowly out, and then the other leg, until he resembles a gymnast on the horse, balanced on his heels and fingers, ready to kick himself loose and pivot in a perfect angle of ninety degrees, a shape of muscled grace. Instead, saying "*Ah!*" he moves his fingers back—walks them back as if they were feelers searching out danger or prey—and lets his stiff back follow them along the unpainted stone floor until, grunting and sighing, he is prone, his hands beside his trunk, his legs together and straight, his eyes looking up at the unfinished wood of his storeroom.

The bell at the street door rings. He closes his eyes and sees two figures swinging from the blackness at the door. He opens them and the door rings once again to say that someone closed it—from outside his threshold or in? He closes his eyes. He promises himself that he will sleep if he is left alone. If no one has come in, he will clench his eyes and sleep and wake refreshed and uncrate books and sell them and after dinner at night he will not watch television; he will stalk his wife through the evening and force up her passions as if she were a sullen child he might edge into laughter, first, and then glad sleep. His back will never hurt again like this. His back will never be separate from him again. He will not be broken apart, he will not be caught like this on the floor of his store, embarrassed in his own place, betrayed by his body that has tried, all early morning, to leave him.

A woman calls "Hello?"

He closes his eyes, the clear plastic figures swing to headlessly face him. He opens his eyes, then closes them, like a child who tries not to smile while faking sleep: the eyes flutter, he feels them roll at the soft lids, he commands them to be still but feels them jump in treason. He makes his breath come evenly, as if a grownup watches him, as if he will be left to really sleep if he thinks he looks as if he really sleeps.

"Hello?"

It is the voice of a local woman, nasal and hard, this upstate small city's voice. No one reads here anyway, and never a babe with a voice like that. She probably wants a phone. Well we don't loan our phones. There's a phone at the Texaco. And we don't have a public john, either. There's a john at the Texaco. Probably there's a bookstore at the Texaco too. Maybe I'm on the floor at the Texaco, how should I know. Put me up on the lifts and see if I'm really all there. And a lube job, please. Well, why don't you change the oil, too? Do bookstore sleepers use a straight, say, ten-weight oil, or would they take a multipurpose mixture—maybe ten dash thirty?

"Hello?"

The voice is closer and he closes his eyes so hard he sees a spurt of rainbow, as if he's punctured a sac of colors inside his lid and they're running down the eyeball onto his cheek.

"Hello? Oh God Jesus *help*! Help!"

He opens his eyes but cannot move his head to the side because of the pain in his back. He says to the ceiling "Hold it. Madam? Hold it, I'm not dead. Shh. I'm not a corpse, madam. Easy—I was resting. Okay? I was resting here."

She says only "Oh."

"Yes."

"Oh."

"I'm sorry I scared you."

"Yes. Well I'm sorry I disturbed your, ah, rest. I only wanted—well I don't think you have—"

"No" he says. "Please. Why don't you go back to the front of the store and I'll be right with you. I was resting." He feels his blush so intensely that he closes his eyes. Then, fearing that she will think him dead again, or dying of a stroke, or sick with some slow poison, or a drunk, or mad, he opens his eyes and smiles through the heat of his skin to say "Please. Would you do that?"

And, when he hears her rubber soles scuffing in the front, near the small best-seller table and the wall of paperbacks, he works at standing up. He rolls slowly to his right, and quickly jabs his left hand like a stiff pincer to the floor behind him. He moans with the pain and her footsteps shuffle, as if she would return to help. He gags "Oh no, just fine, we'll be right there now." He pushes with the fingers of his left hand and his body goes over and he is face down on his floor. The pain in his kidneys is spreading, he can feel it move. The pain is like a stain on paper, or a powder in solution in a plastic corpse: he sees it widen and lengthen and penetrate the secret crevices. Fearing that he takes too long he says "We're on our way."

But he cannot move. He cannot raise his head to call again because the pain has climbed his spine and swells his neck now. His face is crushed to the floor, all of its weight on his right cheekbone, the right nostril grazing the coldness of concrete. As he realizes this he feels the pain rush like a heavy fluid to the cheekbone and the nose. He wants to weep. He wants to ask the customer for help. He wants to go to sleep and wake up painless, or at least on his feet. As if he is walking toward her he says "Now what was it you were interested in?" Like heavy fluid bursting through, the pain comes down his right cheekbone as a leakage of tears. "How can we help you now?" he says.

He sees her shoes beside him, ripple-sole plain brown leather. He sees ankles too slender and calves that are nearly too thick, and then she is bending beside him and, like jump-cut instants of commercial, he has seen her knee and thigh. He closes his eyes. His skin beats. He says "Please. Please."

"Shall I call a doctor? Really—"

"I'm not sick."

"Listen to me. Can you understand what I'm saying?"

"God, of course, of course, of *course*. You think I'm some kind of drunk?"

"Do you hear what I'm saying? Who is your doctor?"

"Lady, I am not a drunk. Not drunk. Not sick. Not dead. Nothing. None of that, understand?"

"I have to call a doctor for you. Or an ambulance, maybe."

"Don't you *hear*?"

"Can you tell me where it hurts?"

"Lady, don't you listen to people?"

"Can you tell me where it hurts?"

He weeps, then, and closes his eyes as if at last he would sleep. The weeping doesn't stop, it gets so loud that he listens in amazement. When he tries to talk he stammers like a child who is caught in the coils of his tantrum, and all he can say is "Back. Bah-bah-back."

With great precision she slowly exaggerates her words to say "You've hurt your *back*. Your *back* hurts? Is that right? You've hurt your *back*?"

"I wanna stand up."

"No, you have to lie there now. Now you lie still, don't worry. That's a good boy. Lie still. Will you do that for me?"

"I wanna stand up. Oh please."

"I'll go call a doctor now and you don't move. You're not supposed to move now. Right? Don't move. I'll go call a doctor for you, that's my boy, and you don't move."

The panic in her voice, its wobble in pitch, the quavers up and down on the cords of her throat, are somehow reassuring to him: if she doesn't know about what has seized and pinned him here, then maybe there is nothing to cope with except in his insides; the problem may be private yet. His sobbing slows, and he says "Please, I beg of you." His chest heaves up—down at the floor—for breath and his throat goes *huff-ha-huff*. He says "I truly deeply beseech," and he knows that a word like "beseech" is never used by hysterics or fall-down drunks. Happily, then, he says "I beseech thee, madam—I mean, I beseech you. Please. Don't call anybody. Please. I've hurt my back rather badly, but I don't think there's any danger at all. I acted silly because I was embarrassed."

"Well you don't need to be embarrassed if you hurt yourself."

He imagines this hard nasal voice with a hundred similar voices at a Christian Council summer camp, or a Board of Planners forum on the sewage plant, or at a meeting of dissidents who want a more meaningful P.T.A. He hears it telling people why they should or shouldn't feel the way they do or do not feel. He wonders if her breasts are veined, and why she sounds as if she has no age, and whether she would scream of excrements while making love, and whether she would let her lover see her whole body flattened in bed like a white map, and whether she makes love at all.

"Thank you" he says. "This must have been horrible for you."

"I was very frightened."

"I'm sorry."

"It was like a nightmare, seeing you."

"I felt like that too. I'm very sorry."

"But you're all right now?"

"I think I will be."

"Well."

"You were tremendously good to try and help me."

"Well. Should I just, I don't know, *leave* you here?"

"Would you mind?"

"Couldn't I get you anything? For your back? Do you take anything for it?"

"I don't know, I never had this."

Her hand rests lightly on his back and his body shivers. She says "Did I hurt you? I'm so sorry."

"No, not at all, you're very kind. You're very kind."

"Here, at least—you must never underestimate these, they're really wonderful medicines. Here." And her small fingers, hesitantly, and then almost with the force of anger—grownup's anger at the child who is sick and cannot name his sickness—force at his lips. "Excuse me, but really, they can really help you a lot."

Her aspirin is on his tongue like flour, caking and drying the moisture of his membranes, settling into a lump, beginning to burn. He works his tongue, swallows and swallows, crushes his tongue at the roof of his mouth, chokes and starts to cough. He kicks his foot and moans and her fingers return, bringing the odor of her handbag —lavender and the dry scent of tissues that have soaked in evaporations of cologne, and the resinous perfume of powder from her compact, and pungencies of leather and cloth. She forces in a cube and his tongue works automatically before he identifies the taste as a raspberry Charm. He sucks and churns with his mouth and then sniggers. "I haven't had one of these since I was a kid. I didn't know they made them anymore."

"Now you feel better, don't you?"

He closes his eyes and sees the aspirin inside his gullet. He sees its particles drifting down as if he watched his body, transparent on a dark background, swiveling in the darkness to face him, slumped in his rocking chair, downstairs in his house, keeping his nightly watch. He hears her breathe as she watches him and he is hearing how, while he watches at night, clutched by her dreams sometimes, or by his absence, his wife upstairs might thrash to her narrow back and snore, or grunt loudly enough for him downstairs to look up at the ceiling and look and then look away to the blue-gray light.

He says "Would you call someone for me?" And before she answers he says "I would gladly—I would *want* to give you the book you were after. I would beg you to let me give you that book. I was getting scared and you stopped me and that was a big favor. Would you let me give you the book if we have it in stock?"

"Nonsense" she says. "You don't help someone for payment, do you?"

"But you wouldn't deny me the pleasure of saying thank you?"

"We'll see" she says. "Who would you like me to call?"

"Would you telephone my wife and—this won't embarrass you?"

"After finding a corpse in the back of a bookshop? I don't see how anything could."

"Would you telephone my wife and tell her to unplug the television set?"

"Unplug the television set."

"Would you ask her to do that? Unplug the television set and come down here and give me a hand?"

"She knows how to help this back business of yours?"

"We've never had it before. Yes she does. Would you do that?"

"Well—"

"Unplug the electric book, tell her, and get her ass down here to the shop."

"Oh I couldn't say that to a stranger, could I?"

"No. Well, you tell her any way you can. All right? Tell her *some*thing like that, something approximate?"

"And she knows how to help you up? She knows about this better than a doctor?"

"Better than a doctor."

"All right, then. Yes. I'll get something of your message across."

"You're an angel. Excuse me, but I'm so damned grateful—"

"Nonsense. And stop excusing yourself."

"And you'll let me give you the book?"

She says "Actually" and he closes his eyes, sees them swinging slowly around, their plastic loincloths covering nothing but clearnesses. "Actually, I was looking for an Easter card, I'm afraid. I wanted a card for Good Friday—that's today, you see, our great holy day in our religion. I wanted something I could give my mother for Good Friday. She sets great stock by getting a card from each of her children on Good Friday."

"Card."

"Oh, I do read. I read all the time. Only—"

"Yes" he says. "I'm afraid we don't sell them here."

"I'm so sorry" she says. "I seem to have disappointed you so much. But: that's life, you'll have to forgive me, won't you? What's your number?"

"What?"

"What's your telephone number?"

"Oh. Listen, you might try the Texaco down the street, they might be able to help you."

"Excuse me?"

"Sure."

"Don't you want me to—"

"No."

"No? You don't want me to call for you?"

"No."

"You want me to leave you here like this?"

"If you would."

"But what about your wife?"

He sees them swinging in the darkness, trunks and limbs and clear plastic loincloths. There is no mystery behind the transparent cloths, there is only what he sees—the nothing that is hidden by the un-hiding cloth, and behind it the darkness which they swivel from, side by side and headless, while the music around them jumps and stutters, and the medicine rolls in slowest motion from nowhere to nowhere, in solution, over and over again through the night, while Susan Hayward weeps and in her weeping pauses for their bodies' looming clarity, then weeps again.

SARCOPHAGUS: A TRIBUTE *

On Finding My Photograph Cherished among His Papers

DACHINE RAINER

*This poem is, ex post facto,
for Marion Morehouse Cummings*

Now that eec is dead, there is no one to write poems for you. (If
only I'd thought of it sooner!) Take this. Several lines are yours in
any case, spoken with your own furious anguish, a raging pain
which when you first expressed it, I had yet to experience . . . only
a few cherishing years after. Here, humbly (an enormity of which
you know me incapable, to intend it as substitute; for it was about
the impossibility of substitution that you cried)—but do take this,
Marion. You, having succored me until your own death . . . I am
abandoned, desolate. Dear Buffer State you were to Estlin's poems,
dear, amusing, overly efficient blockade between loathed intrusions
and his muse. How his ambiguities roared! How I envied him; him,
not you. Once, in early days, before you discovered to whom I
belonged, your funny, pointed anecdote, meant to warn me away:
let these verses correct you, as I never would. I wanted interference
run; I never desired to be subject of poems, not even such great
ones, being, as you quickly discovered, as handsomely placed, by
another man, in another art entirely.

How greedily death lunged at them . . . Too late for all things
save memorials . . . which in no way assuages death's appetites . . .

* A sequence from *In Love and Death: E.J.B.*

Now for you, dearest Marion, with gratitude, this minor gift, re-
marking the different kinds of love, of which our friendship was
only a shade less exultant.

I can bear to look now, I had to agree,
admonished by solicitors and the medical profession,
by the former for "bohemian self-indulgence: we must see
where we are," reproached kindly, not without calculated charm
for tending (even in death?) to disregard the importance
of papers, including documents and fiscal statements
and every indication of imminent pauperdom,

as firmly reproved by the doctor for callous indifference
to my own well-being, by which, with misgivings,
a similar concern is presumed for my future competence
as a fee-paying patient.

        All transitions are difficult:
my husband is talking about the articulation
of a woman's wrist in Ingres' "Le Bain Turc."
        . . . *difficult*, I echo, entering his room.

I had looked at his art all this year,
there are fewer drawings here than everywhere in the
        grieving house,
looked with continuity, not as a widow might, nor as his lover,
but as a bewitched critic, in love with his muse,
that Goddess who with mine completed our impassioned
        quadrangular coupling,
a Saskia tolerated cook and inspiration, companion
and unpurchased model, absolutely simultaneously available
In all roles, I now bereft of all, enter his lifeless room.

Valéry's conversations with Degas lay shut upon the table.
In the chair, only my memory
of his fondness for Van Gogh's Yellow Chair
seems to create an Occupier:
        Once in an hotel in Norway,
        I was about to . . . when "No, no!" the proprietor

came running, "You can't sit THERE!
That's Ibsen's chair! SHE
with a teasing nod at my particularity,
is something of an Ibsen. (I had been.)

On the table, his reading glasses, neatly encased,
openly displayed as useless.
I touch his drawing glasses,
clay smudged, which I must never wipe clean again:
If one's eyes went, that would be the end,
but he also said, *The end never comes as expected*
in manner or time.
(So had our unannounced ending been.)

Lumps of clay and smudging stubs of pastels on a shelf,
a last Conté drawing leans unfinished on the chair,
pens and crayons crowd a marmalade jar,
he was working on the final morning.

Life is never completed, only forsaken.

Forsaken
the cloth has dried over the wet clay
like a dusty burial sheet over armature's mysterious shapes,
his sculpture tools fastidiously arrayed into futility,
a work of art is never completed, only abandoned,
as life itself is abandoned incomplete.
I cannot agree that *ripeness is all.*

Drooped over the table, his tattered copy of Clark's "The Nude."
All other books have been removed.
His black portfolios have lost their shabby bulges,
stacked against the wall, look starved blank and empty;
the floor has been tidied of experimental figures
cavorting on newsprint: blue ink studies of one
who solitarily creeps on all fours or flees from his terror,

or coupled soars, flies on a cloud
or is overwhelmed by a wave or caught
in flagrante, in a net,

as Rembrandt's "Vulcan Catches Mars and Venus"
in the web of love (etched
in amusement for us, in solidarity,
caught as we were)!

All living forms vacate the atmosphere
except in two black linen notebooks, sprawled together
where lie huddled the ripened forms,
with the cold hands and living faces of unknown persons.
At the sight of his beloved script
the stone coffin of my heart cracks:
>   D says, "The tongue is a highly fallible instrument
>   of perception." I do not know her least through mine.
>   Further, Tongue's exulting taste, exalted touch,
>   and (almost) smell—"Holy Three in One."
I close the book as though I intrude
on his furrowed pleasures with a previous self.

The room is a mausoleum: bawdiness and gaiety,
I have given his lecherous limericks away
to a petitioner . . . Facility and wisdom.

I am readmonished by the sobriety of solicitors and turn
out the contents of his briefcase and stare
on behalf of my bereaved daughter,
and all others, anxious and impatient at my failure, they say,
to rally from Fate's swift clout, after long delay.

But the sight of his rhythmical prose is more real than marble.
my jagged heart, coffined, terrible—

composed, neatly beribboned papers untied, remain tidy,
obscure to me, one must surmise helpful, as he was.
As he was? in the notebooks most as he was:
take the Celtic strain in a canny Scotsman
's furious note to himself about treacherous offspring,
with its acrostic summation named: Ian,
a man may smile and smile and be a villain.
As he is, this note to himself . . . his sketches,
drawings, a prose reminder and sexy verses . . .

but I must return to these papers
where flights of his commercial calculations
rise Debussy-like, like lyrical quarter notes

Debussy! the very name is like a tone
from the living sands of the unquenchable sea
which conversations with a "late" friend amplify
(for me, too, as for him, our dearest friends are "late,"
their flourishing words untouchable, remote:
    "How he longed to hear *Pelléas*,
    Your glorious voice, your interpretation," murmuring . . .

    "Grazie, grazie, if you knew how I too miss him"
    "And so I thought, I will listen intently for two
    (almost like pregnancy, not death)
    and at the rehearsals you know I did"
    "Ah, I know . . ."
        "but inside the gold and red Garden
    the jewels and chandeliers, perfumes and velvet opulence of
        an Opening
    all that sensuality of setting and sound—"

    "—before the music began?"
    "Yes. It suddenly grew dark and cold like the going of the
        sun.
    I felt his absence near me like a presence.
    Deaf even to that swollen disturbance of strings,
    I knew I was—I *was*—dead"
    and our gentle friend confirming thoughtfully,
    "part of you is, it is indeed, is dead, died when he did . . ."

Conversations meander and fade . . .
We heard the pained *recitative* of M ascend:
    "You must be lonely I was told when C died,
    by everyone—editors, publishers, pen pals and just plain
    friends (and I was baby how I was) and their invitations
    and consolations poured in. But I wasn't lonely for them.
    I was lonely for him."

One begins to understand the Hindu widow's pyre
or, perhaps the perpetual mourning of Queen Victoria.
    "Carry on," M's harsh mimicry, "for *him*
    and edit his journals and so on and on . . .
    but I don't want to be distracted, I who have been loved . . .

Mutilated by fate . . . a widow is an amputee . . . a voice remarked.

If only . . . had I known . . . my regrets tumble and abound
    "You ain't goin' in for all that atone
    talk or what's the point of . . . ?" a farther voice remotely.
Like what's the point of art when we can't see the meaning
of life? I rushed headlong. What *is*?
    "One day I open my eyes; the next day I shut them,
    I believe *inbetween* matters. So do you . . ."
    his dark voice circled widening rings inside a dead room.

    I sat at my husband's late desk
    listening to such mellifluous voices
    of our departed friends,
    turning the pages
    of his forceably silenced voice.

    The rain which used to grow us, rots you,
    the sun which warmed, bleaches,
    dissects flesh from bone,
    artist, volatile element,
    I long hugely to embrace your fate.
The paper work began again:
I undid the cherished foldings
(his hands had touched these ribbons)
when O! the start of recognition,
I, smiling, looking out lively at this vanishing hull,
myself consoling me, as this image, tucked away
among brochures and forms, had comforted him:

I, once gay, secure, incomprehensibly loved, free.
    A quick transition of his view of me opposed itself
    to mine of him, and I was overcome
    borne away by a sensual poignancy:

his low voice, elegant hands, the Grecian back
of his young neck, his unclothed stance
the Youth of Subiaco, his charmed words, the favours
      of Valéry.
A sealed document, prompting no curiosity
then, irrelevant and out of order, our few letters
(we were seldom apart). "As Donne to his wife, I to you:
    The sun is dim and cold in your absence,
    moons wane, seas dry, the gate of heaven creaks shut,
    Time stands. Hurry back, fly!"
and down the page, tucked wryly: "I faint, I fail, I die."

    Suffused by your love for me,
    I loved myself momentarily
    as I had not all this year of your death,
    only to feel again, more deeply alone.
The photograph smiled on and on.

    Inconceivably, you had said,
    You must take another lover: I will not live forever.
    When the time comes . . . as though you were
        reminding me
    of the most perfunctory of necessities
    and not some vast incongruity like:
    "Did you remember to wind the clock?" in the center
        of passion.

    Remember. Sternly. Be obedient.
    I will not, I had said airily.
    You will live forever. We had left it at that.
Hard by my stiffly smiling photograph
your bearded passport, an ominous camouflage, slips by.

I remove a practical-looking sheaf of papers
with which to gratify any solicitor.
    Then, thrusting this rough draft with the rest,
    (all our short history belongs together;
    if you are anywhere, you will know what I am about).
The briefcase closed tight,
I quietly shut the door, and withdraw to another room, to wait.

SEVEN POEMS

CAROL TINKER

1

struck and calm
i want what you want
a calm
empty days and
cumulative energy like thought
forgetting

2
wet green hallelujahs

casket
of leaf green
            hallelujahs
the heart of the wait's
got singly
binderies of books
and closet queens and
anger with
            nothing anger
settled period

as no moving
        like hard rain
lying at the feet of the
wet green
       hallelujahs

3

the tissue sent with
vision the integrity of
carcinoma of tons of flesh
of bones of bellies nail parings
burning in an ashtray

here's a dog
drill down
unconnected sound sending
  the frets go dark
    goldbeater's membrane

through which
  he's standing talking not me

die two at a time arbutus
smell it   a white noon
assimilate the female principle
not a
love story

4

yes, sam johnson,

     "prodigious noble wild prospects"

but christ
i feel like ned kelly
looking down from
buena vista heights
on the city—

       frisco in the lotus
       your pluck hung high
       your veins opened

       the halitus of haight street
       rises with incense
       this cold morning

5
buddha's birthday

                in memory of martin luther king, jr.

come & see   you
have shown me
passion

wind blows the eucalyptus
and sun shines through
in the panhandle
prime among others
         my moving eye

april the fourth month
new spring gardens:
dogwood flowers on lower market street

buddha's birthday

requiem mass for brother martin
 we circumambulate the cathedral and the pacific union club

passover
      easter

or in the revelation of john:

       nevertheless i have somewhat against thee
       because thou hast left thy first love

       the venerable bede
       knew of the wolf
       taught his paternoster
       by monks
       all he could say
       was lamb,
                  lamb

6
thank you capitalism for the expanding universe

o tucumcari lady took good care of you
tucumcari lady made you free
roast dog and fat tobacco tea

says
i'm better than a restaurant
comforted with scalpels, peeling
off a billboard
laughing in the stretcher
happy in the bread machine
                 reclaimed from greyhound

pure mind knows
she broke you
of riots and spreading diseases
so that all your clothes are washed forever
so that you could stand here naked

cellists!   pomos!   fleas!
mary pestered by angels!
hermes nude on washday his finger in the dyke!

it is hard   it is duty

tucumcari took good care of you
it's that history
got you busted

7
Ishtar, or the explosion in a shingle factory

growing
        growing
i'm gagging on jelly
doughnuts full of nitroglycerine
to steady the heart
which is in a peculiar spasm

i've got apples and
you don't

my hand covers the characters and
smears them as i write and
i write large now
to make something of myself
fingernail parings, flaking skin,
hair combings
dry dead cells settle from the air
faded but without blemish

they wanted to know if it's poetry
or is it a black flag

boys see more dead cats
than girls; write
bloodier letters

hard brown sugar sticks
in the bowl
i mean i'm trying to
claw it out with this
menorah of burning fingers

THE SULTAN'S LITTLE
HARUM-SCARUM

or: An Apocryphal Sequel to *The Lustful Turk**

EDUOARD RODITI

For his imperial harem, one of our sultans once acquired a pe-
culiarly unsuitable young Infidel wife who yet turned out to be—
for such are the devious ways of Fate—a veritable godsend, for a
while, to our glorious Empire. She was an English girl, the or-
phaned daughter of a professor of biblical archaeology at Oxford
University who had once been a very controversial figure in Angli-
can Church circles, where the fruits of his historical research often
supplied ammunition to those divines who were concerned with
what, in those days, was still called "the Higher Criticism."

This unfortunate Professor, a widower, foolishly allowed his
golden-haired child, then barely twelve years old, to accompany
him on an expedition to the upper reaches of the Euphrates, where
he planned to conduct excavations in a very wild and lonely region
which he believed to be the actual site of the legendary Garden of
Eden, though it had now degenerated, since times immemorial, into
an arid and mountainous landscape where rocks and ravines might
remind one more readily of an Earthly Hell than of an Earthly
Paradise. There, from the rediscovered kitchen middens of our
common ancestors, the professor hoped to recover fossilized human

* See the explanatory note on page 173.

turds. Properly analyzed in a geological laboratory, these would subsequently allow dieticians specialized in the palaeontology of the quaternary to identify the undigested but petrified remains of whatever grasses and roots or nuts and fruits had provided the staples of the diet of Adam and Eve until they had both eaten of the Forbidden Fruit, which, of course, they had digested and excreted elsewhere, after their immediate expulsion from the Garden of Eden.

In the course of this expedition, however, the professor's party was attacked by Kurdish bandits who raped and slaughtered them all, with the single exception of the distinguished archaeologist's golden-haired daughter. A natural respect for her tender years and for her market value as an unsullied exotic virgin prevented her captors from allowing her to witness the orgy and massacre in the course of which the rest of the party perished. Only later was the child told, by a village gossip, how her bespectacled and white-haired father had been disguised as a bearded Bedouin beldame and forced to execute a belly dance in order to rouse the baser instincts of the rabble at whose hands he was destined to perish after satisfying their ignoble desires. Though the child was spared no detail of this hideous account, she never believed a word of it.

For the next couple of years, this future inmate of the imperial Harem was kept closely guarded in a Kurdish mountain village, where her very identity was concealed, for fear of reprisals. Then, one summer, a dread disease infected the Kurdish tribe's flocks. Deprived overnight of more than half of their only legitimate riches, the tribesmen, unable to subsist on occasional banditry in an area that all wise travelers had learned to circumvent, decided to sell for a stiff price their only negotiable asset, the golden-haired virgin who lived in their midst.

Her name had originally been Gladys Tibbs, something both meaningless to Kurds and difficult to pronounce. Her captors therefore renamed her Aysheh bent Hakim, having ascertained that she was the daughter of a man of learning, and it was under this new name that Gladys was now offered, through a number of reliable and specialized intermediaries, as a Kurdish princess who would be a suitably beautiful and high-born wife for the Imperial Seraglio.

Aysheh, *née* Gladys Tibbs, immediately saw in this audacious plan a rare chance to escape from the dreary social and cultural life of a Kurdish mountain village where nobody was at all interested in identifying the site of the legendary Garden of Eden or, for that matter, in any other subject that might have been discussed, over tea and mustard-and-cress sandwiches, in a learned Oxford drawing room. She indeed turned out to be far more co-operative than her Kurdish captors expected. She explained to them, for instance, that a recent French invention now made it possible to produce at short notice reliably lifelike portraits which, though grey because the camera was still color-blind, could subsequently be colored by hand. Enquiry then revealed that the great Paris photographer Nadar already had qualified former pupils, the brothers Abdallah, in Constantinople and Cairo, where they had been appointed "photographers of His Imperial Highness the Sultan and of His Royal Highness the Khedive." Brought to Constantinople by the intermediaries to whose care she had been entrusted, Aysheh posed for a photograph in the Pera studio of Abdallah Frères, after which her portrait was exquisitely colored by a miniaturist who was a nun in the Convent of Notre Dame de Sion, where she conducted art classes for the daughters of wealthy Infidels, who are not forbidden by their faith to reproduce the human figure.

Because the womenfolk of the Kurds and of the Berbers are known, however modest in other respects, to reveal their features more freely than their Turkish, Persian, or Arab sisters, it was not considered unduly daring to communicate to the Sultan this un-veiled likeness of his proposed bride. Other circumstances conspired moreover to crown with success the plans of the Kurdish bandits. The Sultan himself, an enlightened monarch who had visited England in his boyhood, was now seeking a solution to the Kurdish problem, which was a constant thorn in the side of the Sublime Porte. He had thus come to believe that the addition of a Kurdish princess to his staff of official wives might well serve as a means of assuring himself greater loyalty among her turbulent compatriots in the distant mountains of eastern Anatolia. It thus came to pass that Aysheh bent Hakim, *née* Gladys Tibbs, found herself confined, far sooner than she had expected, to the strict but luxurious seclusion of the Imperial Seraglio.

She had originally planned, in her ignorance of our Moslem marriage rites and Imperial etiquette, to reveal her identity to the unsuspecting Sultan during their courtship, perhaps on the occasion of their first moment of relative privacy. Her English upbringing and her subsequent experience of the somewhat rustic and relaxed customs of Kurdish village life prevented her from foreseeing that, no sooner said than done, she would be the lawful wife of the Sultan on their very first meeting, so that she was quite taken by surprise when she discovered that her first moment of privacy with her Lord and Master was granted to her only on the occasion of her official bridal night.

She was prepared for this solemn occasion by a whole staff of palace eunuchs, some of them hairdressers, masseurs, cosmeticians or costumers, others instructors in deportment or etiquette. The latter rehearsed her mercilessly until she had mastered every modest gesture, every coy glance, every tender word and every passionate sigh that should accompany her voyage from maidenhood to womanhood. Never before had she seen such a fuss made of any event in her young life. Actually, she rather enjoyed all this flim-flamflummery. At last, carefully coached and adorned, she was led into the Sultan's private apartments. There, as soon as the door was closed by an armed eunuch who would stand outside all night in order to watch over the safety of the Caliph of all the Faithful, she fell prostrate at the latter's feet and exclaimed, in her perfect Oxford English: "Your Imperial Majesty must be informed, before it is too late, that His most humble servant's real name is Gladys Tibbs. I'm the daughter of the late professor of biblical archaeology at Oxford University! He was killed by the Kurds, on an expedition to find fossilized turds . . ."

She expected this announcement, which was alien to everything that the eunuchs had so carefully taught her, to have almost miraculous effects on the Sultan. As a matter of fact it did, though scarcely those that she had hoped to witness. Instead of promptly raising his supplicant new bride from the carpet on which she grovelled and then magnanimously liberating her from her marriage in order to entrust her to the care of the British ambassador, who would send her back to her long-lost Oxford home or to the girls' school in Eastbourne where her education had been interrupted by her accompanying her late father on his infelicitous expedition, the astonished Sultan exclaimed, with a perfect Oxford drawl:

"Tibbs? Did you say Tibbs? Are you the daughter of that old fool who instructed me in English when he was in Constantinople some twenty years ago with the British Archaeological Mission? Do you really mean to say that he was actually able to seduce and marry a Kurdish princess when he finally left us to go on the

expedition from which he returned a few months later with the
fossilized rudder of Noah's Ark? You little harum-scarum, you
can't make me believe any such hocus-pocus. Old Tibbs may be a
wizard at identifying fossils, but he would never have been capable
of begetting a beautiful daughter like you. And since when do
Kurdish princesses enjoy the privilege of being brought up by Eng-
lish governesses in their wild mountain retreats? There's something
fishy, I admit, in all this, but we'll get to the bottom of it in due
time, Tibbs or fibs, Kurds or fossilized turds . . ."

Argue as she might, poor Princess Aysheh, *née* Gladys Tibbs,
failed that fateful night to convince the Sultan of her real identity.
The more she appealed to his better self, the more she confused
him with her unlikely tale of woe. She even roused his passions, till
he finally insisted on enjoying his conjugal rights then and there
with so beautiful and fanciful an English-speaking Kurdish prin-
cess. Finally, she was forced to yield to his advances and soon
became his favorite wife, partly because she was the only one who
had ever resisted his demands and forced him to woo her, partly
because he could chatter with her in English about a great variety
of subjects that transcended the intellectual level of his other wives
and concubines.

After a while, however, she managed to convince him of her real
identity. To avenge her father, the Sultan then sent a military
expedition which successfully pacified the bandit-infested moun-
tains of the upper reaches of the Euphrates Valley, even recovering
from the robbers the late professor's collection of rare fossil turds,
which you may now see displayed in a glass case in our National
Archaeological Museum, though some of them have also been sent,
as a memorial to the martyr's scholarship, to the Ashmolean Mu-
seum in Oxford. But the Sultan and his pseudonymously Kurdish
wife had meanwhile fallen in love. Instead of returning to complete
her education at an Eastbourne boarding school for the daughters
of gentlemen, Princess Aysheh, *née* Gladys Tibbs, had decided to
remain, for better or for worse, in the harem of her Imperial
spouse.

Whenever she entered her Lord and Master's apartments for
their nightly trysts, he would now greet her tenderly as his Little
Harum-scarum, after which they would reminisce a while about
happy days spent in distant England, where the Sultan had spent a
few summers as a schoolboy, to perfect his English. While he then

boasted of his batting scores in village cricket matches or of his prowess as a fast bowler, she would talk nostalgically of mustard-and-cress sandwiches and of lemon-cheese pies served at garden parties in the rural parsonages of Oxfordshire, after which they would settle down happily to the more serious business of the evening.

In due time, the Sultana Aysheh, *née* Gladys Tibbs, thus became the real power behind the Peacock Throne, especially when she became pregnant and gave birth to a young prince, unlike the Sultan's other wives who had all borne him only daughters. By that time, the Sultan's Little Harum-scarum had also come to the conclusion that her fate, howevermuch it might have raised storms of protest or released cascades of tearful pity among unmarried feminists in Cheltenham or Leamington Spa, was much more brilliant than it would have been had she married a monogamous young Oxford scholar, as she once might have expected, in fact some brilliant disciple of her late father, a young archaeologist specialized in identifying the historical sites of somewhat legendary events related in the Old Testament. She might thus have married, for instance, the world-famous discoverer of Jephthah's daughter, buried in an urn on the spot where her heartbroken father had kept his vow and sacrificed her as a burnt offering after his victory, or the equally famous discoverer of the diabolical mandrake root which had grown in the ground where Onan had once impiously spilled his seed.

Though a brilliant young archaeologist's wife may experience great intellectual satisfactions in her conjugal life, when she dazzles her learned guests to a scholarly collation with Chaldaean recipes salvaged by her husband from cuneiform inscriptions that he has deciphered on previously illegible tablets, the intrigues of a great Imperial Harem can offer more scope to the intelligence and initiative of a woman who knows how to utilize her talents and wield her power with real discretion. Since fate had seen fit to grant her such power, the Sultana Aysheh, *née* Gladys Tibbs, decided that she would be truly foolish to refrain from using it, not so much to her own advantage as to that of her sex and of mankind at large.

Her education, before her Kurdish adventures, had not been neglected. In addition to a good basic knowledge of English constitutional history as explained by Walter Bagehot, she was endowed with sound political notions of her own. On the whole, her ideas were moderately progressive. She had read most of the published novels of Charles Dickens and even *Adam Bede*. Seeking a historical example to inspire and guide her in her self-appointed mission, she was wise enough to understand the peculiarities of her own situation and, instead of setting out to imitate in her actions those of some feminist termagant, she preferred to choose as her model Prince Albert of Saxe-Coburg-Gotha who, as Prince Consort, had so often inspired the wise decisions for which Queen Victoria was destined to be remembered by several generations of her nostalgic and grateful subjects.

More and more, the Sultana Aysheh, *née* Gladys Tibbs, now discussed politics with her Lord and Master. Sometimes, he would heave sighs of boredom as he listened to her; often, at first, he would interrupt her by playfully pinching her shapely bottom in order to recall her to her more pleasurable wifely duties. Still, she seemed to derive healthy satisfactions from these too. Little by little, the Sultan learned to appreciate her political acumen and began to come to her for advice in solving some of the problems of his far-flung empire. Their Imperial evenings would then be spent discussing the latest editorial of the London *Times* which speculated on how the Sublime Porte would respond to a recent diplomatic move of the Ballhausplatz, or on whether "the Sick Man of Europe" would be able to withstand some new military pressure of the Russian Steamroller in the Balkans or the Caucasus; after which, having solved at least in theory the problems of the day, the Sultan and his Little Harum-scarum would settle down to such lighter pastimes as an old-fashioned Cockney "slap and tickle" or, if they needed first to rouse their appetites, to a joint reading of *The Lustful Turk* or of an English translation of a French classic of its kind, *The Memoirs of a Masseuse*.

All too often, the Gallicisms of the latter, which had been hurriedly translated by a slovenly hack, perplexed them and led them astray in the *selva oscura* of philological speculation. One night, they thus devoted several desultory hours to an *explication de texte*, trying to visualize what might well be meant by the following cryptic paragraph: "In the confusion that ensued, he gamahuched the Duchess behind a palm tree in the conservatory, then begged her to order her footmen to flog him for having failed to respect her. She complied with his wishes, but insisted that he should also gamahuche her French maid, which he proceeded to do to me in the presence of the whole household while he was being roundly chastized for the liberties he had taken. Unperturbed, the Duchess watched us through her lorgnette. . . ."

Gamahuched? The Imperial lovers racked their memories of classical philology and of several contemporary foreign languages without being able to understand what might well be meant by this cryptic word in *The Memoirs of a Masseuse*. Then, a few days later, the Sultan's Little Harum-scarum coyly announced to her Lord and Master that she had solved the riddle. Among the other ladies of the Imperial Seraglio, she had discovered a long-dead Sultan's former concubine, an elderly Armenian lady who, having previously been educated by the French nuns of Notre Dame de Sion, had developed a taste for advanced French poetry and chanced upon this curious word in a somewhat more explicit context, in fact in one of the poems of Paul Verlaine's *Hombres*. When the Sultana Aysheh, *née* Gladys Tibbs, now explained blushingly to the Sultan how he could gamahuche her like any English Duchess or French maid, his Imperial Highness was as surprised as Monsieur Jourdain discovering, in Molière's *Le Bourgeois Gentil-homme*, that what he had just been taught to call "prose" was exactly what he had always been speaking. But a rose, by a new name, can smell much sweeter; and the Imperial couple henceforth gamahuched all the more gleefully.

But this philological episode proved to be the source of sweeping reforms in the Imperial Harem. It occurred to the Sultana Aysheh, *née* Gladys Tibbs, that its numerous ladies wasted all too much of their talents and time on idle occupations, endlessly filing their nails, plucking their eyebrows, playing patience, reading the future from tea leaves or mooning over French novels of doubtful intellectual value. With the approval of her Imperial Lord and Master, the Sultana Aysheh now put them all to work reading the foreign press and drafting intelligence reports. From the nights that he now spent with his Little Harum-scarum, the Sultan returned increasingly refreshed in mind as well as in body. In the audiences that he gave on the morrow, whether to his own viziers, to foreign diplomats, or to petitioners from every class among his subjects, the decisions that he took and the judgments that he pronounced soon began to earn him throughout the world the reputation of a modern Solomon. To the dismayed Russian ambassador, he would quote, with a faint note of sarcasm, what the editorial of the London

Times had recently suggested that a somewhat less debilitated "Sick Man of Europe" might still do to save some threatened Caucasian or Balkan province of our dwindling Empire. To the equally surprised English ambassador, he would almost absent-mindedly mention the latest London Stock Exchange quotations for Suez Canal shares, thus revealing that he too had been wisely nibbling at the hard-pressed Egyptian khedive's fabulous holdings of this stock, which Prime Minister Disraeli, through his Rothschild connections, was seeking to acquire *en bloc* and at a discount for the British Crown.

But the Imperial Harem soon found itself understaffed as a camouflaged intelligence agency, and the Sultana Aysheh, *née* Gladys Tibbs, was forced to seek ways and means of recruiting new talent for its rapidly expanding activities. Increasingly staffed with bespectacled bluestockings recruited from among the underemployed feminists of all Western Nations, it was rapidly losing much of its glamor as a legendary abode of odalisques and houris. In London, the realist novelist George Gissing, seeking in the main reading room of the British Museum the real-life material that he could use in *The New Grub Street*, began to observe that this great reservoir of exploited female intellectual talent was already haunted by far fewer "odd women" of the kind that generally eke out a meager subsistence there as "ghosts" for more eminent male scholars. On the other hand, the halls of such learned clubs as the Athenaeum were more and more deserted as their members, for lack of female help, were increasingly reduced to doing their own dreary spadework in the main reading room of the British Museum. In Moscow and Saint Petersburg, the ranks of those feminist Nihilists whose activities the great novelist Joseph Conrad had so well described in *Under Western Eyes* were likewise thinning. Fewer of them could now be found to conceal time bombs beneath their bustles and, in a flurry of hastily raised petticoats, to bowl them unerringly into the passing carriages of reactionary ministers of police. In the emergency, a new kind of miniaturized time bomb had to be devised, small enough to be concealed in a man's bowler hat. In Vienna, the more intellectual Catholic orders were experiencing difficulty in recruiting novices for their convents among the convert daughters of titled Jewish bankers. In Paris, slim volumes of Symbolist poems published on green paper by Lesbian poetesses at their own expense became increasingly scarce. From all over

Europe, a secret network of Turkish agents was indeed recruiting young women of education, intelligence, and talent for our Sultan's Harem, where they were immediately put to work reading newspapers and more specialized periodicals or writing press reviews and intelligence reports, but in far greater comfort and luxury than they had previously known in the British Museum, in the Bibliothèque Nationale or elsewhere. As for our Sultan, the Ruler of all the Faithful, he was now the best informed of all caliphs since Haroun-al-Rashid, in fact the wisest of all living monarchs.

Almost overnight and by purely peaceful means, the "Sick Man of Europe" had become a great progressive power, feared and respected in Whitehall, by the Ballhausplatz, the Quai d'Orsay, the Wilhelmstrasse, and on the banks of the Neva. When a British engineer invented the submarine and failed to interest the First Lord of the Admiralty in its usefulness as a guarantee of world peace, the diligent bespectacled odalisques of our Imperial Seraglio promptly brought the matter to the attention of our Sultan; and so it came to pass that the Imperial Turkish Navy was the first in the world to order and commission submarines. In France, our political propaganda brought about a literary revolution: working on our secret payroll, the popular novelist Pierre Loti deliberately gave his foolish readers the false impression that the ladies of our harems had nothing better to do than to entertain him secretly to coffee, idle talk, and *rahat loukoum*. For a while, the Quai d'Orsay thus continued to believe that it could successfully undermine our authority among the Christians of Syria and Lebanon.

But our moral rearmament as a great power was thwarted all too soon by the sinister intrigues of our imperialist enemies. Puzzled at first by a secret drain on England's female intelligence, which was already threatening the future of the English novel and was diverting younger bluestockings from the goose-quill pens that had made George Eliot and Mrs. Gaskell world famous, Scotland Yard began to watch more carefully the activities of our agents who were so busy recruiting talent for the Imperial Harem. Oddly enough, these agents, unlike their fictional colleagues in that hoary classic of English erotic fantasy, *The Lustful Turk*, seemed to lay no store by good looks, nor indeed by unsullied virtue; indeed, the passport to employment, wherever these young women vanished, appeared to be intelligence and experience rather than innocence and beauty. Yet those who could be traced after their disappearance all wrote

from the same Imperial palaces built on the shores of the Golden
Horn or the Bosphorus, from Top Kapou, Dolmah Bahtche, Bey-
lerbey, or Yildiz. Our Sultan thus began to be suspected of having
very peculiar tastes and of being the only client of a White Slave
Traffic of an entirely novel kind.

To uncover its methods and purposes, Scotland Yard soon found
a suitable agent: Miss Gwendolen Trollope, an unemployed elderly
lady archaeologist of formidable appearance who, for many years,
had been reader and research assistant to the late Professor Tibbs
and, since his mysterious disappearance, had been living in penuri-
ous retirement in a boardinghouse in Bloomsbury. She was
promptly put to work in the British Museum reading room, where,
to attract the attention of the mysterious recruiters, she was in-
structed to read assiduously the more learned publications of the
Prussian Academy of Arts and Sciences. Within a week, Miss
Gwendolen Trollope had been approached by a mild-mannered
Dissenting clergyman and had vanished too.

In a recognition scene similar to that, in classical tragedy, where
Orestes suddenly finds himself about to be sacrificed, in the temple
of Tauris, by his own long-lost sister Iphigenia, the Sultana Aysheh,
née Tibbs, found herself facing, a few weeks later, her own late
father's former research assistant, when Miss Gwendolen Trollope
turned up as a Trojan horse, in fact disguised as a new recruit for
the Imperial Harem's secret corps of information specialists. Little
did the Sultana suspect, at the time, what troubles would soon be
brewing, though she wisely refrained from revealing to Miss Trol-
lope her real identity.

Prepared for the very worst and ready to sacrifice her all for the
future of England, Miss Trollope was convinced that she was
doomed, in spite of her age and her appearance, which had never
been at all enticing, to meet at the hands of the Sultan the fate that,
in the eyes of most English women, is worse than death, in fact the
kind of delicious humiliation that is so well described again and
again in the pages of The Lustful Turk, which she had managed to
consult, in the Inferno of the British Museum Library, before set-
ting forth on her perilous mission. As the weeks went by without
her yet having had to submit to any humiliation of the kind that
she both feared and ardently desired, she began to regret her
Bloomsbury boardinghouse, the British Museum main reading
room, in fact her whole drab life of penurious retirement from

which she had escaped to this veritable hive of intellectual activity. Politics had never interested her. Under the scholarly guidance of Professor Tibbs, she had exercised her intellect on problems of an entirely different nature. Originally an amateur collector of geological specimens culled during her girlhood holidays in Wales, in the Lake District, or the Trossachs, she had gradually become an expert in fossilized ferns, petrified woods, and other such prehistoric curiosities. Actually, she could pride herself on having been the one who had originally opened the eyes of Professor Tibbs to the inherent scientific possibilities of fossilized human turds as clues to the diet of prehistoric man.

Reports on Austrian troop movements in Bosnia and Herzegovina left her cold. Her idle emotions began to crystallize in the most peculiarly violent resentments which she even had the courage to voice among her colleagues. Within a few months, Miss Gwendolen Trollope thus became the leader of a movement for feminine rights among the less-satisfied bluestockings of the Imperial Harem, who felt that the Sultan was neglecting them as wives or concubines. After all, they had abandoned the monogamous world of the West and adopted the Moslem way of life, but without yet having enjoyed the more tangible advantages of polygamy. Their murmurs were soon voiced as overt complaints. With the eloquence of a dedicated suffragette leader, Miss Gwendolen Trollope managed to rouse her followers to a real frenzy. One day, when the Sultan was passing through the main reading room of his Seraglio, accompanied by the Sultana Aysheh, *née* Tibbs, a group of infuriated and bespectacled lady scholars, led by Miss Gwendolen Trollope, suddenly rose from their desks and rushed at him, like the maenads attacking Orpheus. In their desperate fight to be joined with him in carnal union, they tore the unfortunate Ruler of All the Faithful limb from limb, trampling to death his faithful Little Harumscarum, who sought in vain to protect the poor Turk from this wild band of lustful Englishwomen.

Scotland Yard, the Foreign Office, and the Colonial Office had won their battle to protect the land route to India against any recovery of the "Sick Man of Europe" as a major political power. In the Honors List that Prime Minister Disraeli proposed to Queen Victoria that year on the occasion of Her Majesty's Birthday, Miss Gwendolen Trollope was the first woman to be awarded the title of Dame of the British Empire.

But Miss Gwendolen Trollope was no longer of this world to enjoy such honors. The palace guards, alarmed by the turmoil, had rushed into the Harem, though too late to protect their Sovereign. They had then arrested the ringleader of the revolt, together with her whole band of rebels. Summarily tried, they were all condemned to be disposed of in a manner which, however barbarous it may seem, has traditionally proven effective as a means of silencing rebellious wives. Each one of them was placed in a stout barrel lined with iron spikes. Over one hundred of these barrels were then allowed to roll down the hills of Bebek into the Bosphorus.

From the heights where the Americans subsequently built Roberts College, the captain of the Palace Guard was able to see that all the barrels sank into the waters, with one exception, which proved that its inmate was a witch. Floating into the Sea of Marmara and then through the Hellespont into the Aegean Sea, this barrel subsequently drifted all the way across the Mediterranean to Gibraltar, where it was salvaged as flotsam and jetsam, in fact as property of her Majesty the Queen. When it was opened, it was found to contain the miraculously pickled and preserved remains of the late Miss Gwendolen Trollope, Dame of the British Empire. Two years after her disappearance, she was moreover identified by the fossilized human turd which, mounted in gold as a pendant, she still wore on a chain round her neck: a famous Bond Street jeweller was able to testify that it was the only bauble of its kind, having been specially made for her, with her initials inscribed in its gold setting, as a gift from the late Professor Tibbs, shortly before his mysterious disappearance. In addition, the lorgnette that was found intact in a rotting leather case in the same barrel proved to have been made for Miss Gwendolen Trollope by a reputable firm of Regent Street opticians, who were able to testify that she was the only one, among their many clients, to have ever required this particular prescription. Like most witches, not only did she float on water instead of sinking like any honest woman, but she had also been for many years an optometrical freak, shortsighted in one eye and farsighted in the other, in fact swivel-eyed enough to have attracted the attention not only of Scotland Yard but of Satan himself.

EXPLANATORY NOTE: The authorship of The Lustful Turk, *ever since its first anonymous publication in London in 1818, has again and again inspired research and speculation among specialists of nineteenth-century English fiction. A felicitous recent discovery, in the somewhat chaotic archives of the Sublime Porte, now allows us to solve all the problems posed by the authorship of this remarkable novel. As everyone knows, the enemies of our Empire had agreed, in 1817, to stamp out the activities of our gallant privateers who, for centuries, had been zealously liberating unfortunate Christian women from the slavery to which they were generally condemned in their native lands. I need but refer the interested reader to such realistic classics as John Cleland's* Fanny Hill: The Memoirs of a Woman of Pleasure, *George Moore's* Esther Waters, *and Stephen Crane's* Maggy, or a Girl of the Streets; *these books all prove that a woman's life, even in relatively modern times, has not always been a bed of roses among the Infidels.*

Be that as it may, an English fleet commanded by Lord Exmouth bombarded Algiers in 1817 and forced its dey, who was a vassal of our Sultan, to hand over some three thousand refugees, including several hundred foreign women who had found happiness in the dey's harem. As is usual in such cases, many of these "liberated" foreigners were then prevailed upon to publish lurid accounts of their experiences in their Moslem "captivity." The more horrifying these pseudographical memoirs, the more widely they were read.

To put an end to so much malicious anti-Turkish propaganda, our Sultan instructed our ambassador to the Court of Saint James to approach a talented English writer who might be prevailed upon to give a more truthful picture of the life of the privileged inmates of an aristocratic Moslem harem. The great novelist Jane Austen dickered with the idea, but subsequently refused the assignment, arguing that she had too little experience of these matters to be able to write about them convincingly. Sir Walter Scott was too busy, or else too chauvinistic. The Reverend Robert Maturin, the immortal author of Melmoth the Wanderer, *accepted the task, but died in 1824, before he had completed it. His unfinished manuscript then fell into the hands of S—— J——, Esq., who claimed, in the first edition of the book, to be of Magdalen College, Oxford.*

In its present version, The Lustful Turk *still includes a series of letters, from Pedro to Angelo and from Angelo to Pedro, which were obviously written by the Reverend Maturin, who, here as well as in* Melmoth the Wanderer, *could not refrain from giving voice to his anti-Catholic prejudices, even if he had now been commissioned to defend the interests of Islam. But the rest of* The Lustful Turk *is* entirely the work of this mysterious S——— J———, Esq.; one need but read his descriptions of love scenes to realize that he was a masochistic passive homosexual who allowed his own erotic fantasies to dictate to him a number of unrealistic episodes, though our ambassador had originally given to the Reverend Maturin sufficiently detailed testimony, from inmates of our harems, to allow the author of the proposed work to present a more realistic picture of our customs.

When The Lustful Turk *was finally published in its present form, its presumptuous author had the audacity to approach our ambassador with a request for payment, claiming that he had completed the Reverend Maturin's task but had not inherited from the latter, together with his unfinished manuscript, any of the sums that had been advanced to him in order to encourage him to concentrate all his talents on this important and confidential work.*

Our ambassador read The Lustful Turk *and was sensible enough to perceive that the book, in its present form, could only do our cause more harm than good. He answered the author's letter with the wisdom of a veritable King Solomon: he suggested that he might consent to pay for part of the book, if the Pope could also be prevailed upon to pay for the writing of the letters exchanged between Angelo and Pedro. And there the matter seems to have rested.*

All this correspondence, between our ambassador and the various authors approached, as well as with the mysterious S——— J——— Esq., who claimed to be of Magdalen College, Oxford, has now come to light in our Imperial Archives. S——— J——— proves to be a certain Silas Jenkins, a notorious London hack, perhaps even a superannuated male prostitute, whose only knowledge of life in an oriental palace seems to have been gleaned from his early apprenticeship as an assistant to the Prince Regent's notoriously homosexual chief cook in the Brighton Pavilion! As for his connection with Magdalen College, it was tenuous: Silas Jenkins had married a former prostitute and now lived mainly, since his talents failed to feed him, on what she had saved, as a kind of new Mary Magdalene, from the immoral earnings of her ill-spent youth.

A LETTER

DAVID GIANNINI

Each morning means
a midget and a sky against
all previous clouds
Each morning history evaporates
from the eye
Each dawn means
still the first yawn ever
Each morning rouses the glimpse
of all previous time
locked in this present of you
But when morning prepares
private spices to revive
the living-appetite
you continue dozing in your
self you adorable sloth
so hunger eats your appetite
in spite of you
Why because you resist your private midget
who could remedy daylight's judgment
by growing larger than he is
You are not horizontal yet
you are *alive*
Why do you deposit depression
under your hair at night

Morning shudders before it
wakes you it stirs in you
the dying not the live
You treat depression like a landlord
it is only a tenant
The trend of the sun the morning long
extends its gestures to the skeleton
and douses the anemic love of sleep
successfully by being blond
The sun has an amorous imagination
But you will not let it in
You seem to insist you have
a limitless connection with night
a night without attributes
Your intimate hobby is to fabricate
comparisons between you
and everything not you
That is a way of living extinction
You make a metaphor of living
Metaphor means movement
but in you it means
moving in place
I think it's because you detest yourself
You see *you* everywhere a very fractured you
moving like anything
not like you
Yes I think you detest yourself
That is why
your mirror slinks away from you
Yours is the expedient way of sports
But instead of contests between
you and the world
contest the midget in you has
a moldable skull and will and
can be more tall because more alive
more you because less another
To do *that* that is
the difficulty most complete
We have been previous together
You have handled my heart

I have handled your heart
My handled heart held a conference
with my brain and together they
made this attempt to duplicate
myself somewhat
but the words already overripe
I love you and give you this
replica of my thought
letter eyeball heart

EN ROUTE AND RETURN

NAOMI BURTON

When you get the last undercover parking space
   seconds before the deluge,
   is that luck or Divine Providence?
Bumping through thunderheads, bracing for sudden falls,
   produces automatic prayer.
   Is that conditioned reflex or habitual recollection?

Arrangements for changing planes in mid airport
   are courtesy of the Heart Fund, which believes
   in the value of long steady walks.
Whereas
   Restroom mirrors come actuarily sponsored.
   Hurry to the nearest desk and indemnify
   the thin grey thread of life you call your own.
Alimentary decisions assume solemn proportions—
   thousand islands, French, Italian, roquefort,
   all of which turn out to be bright orange.
(*Staggering under the totally untotable,*
   do I head a list of people with whom my companion
   would prefer not to travel?)
Dialling "O" is an unnecessary quirk of the affluent,
   says Ma Bell. But where do the poor find
   House Office Building in a hurry in a torn directory?

"Stepgrandmother" is a mouthful that stops the listener
  cold. But
it's a wise step-grandson who recognizes his
  "Er—grandmother" for who she is.

From above it's easy to see how quickly
  a small cloud passes by
  but down there its shadow
  is a darkness of indeterminate duration.

Found you (You) after much search, almost hidden
  in the square root of liturgy.

There's still a lot of forest and green fields
  as yet unscarred.
May no friendly neighborhood bomber come to our aid
  with smart defensive strikes.

Rain streaming past the window makes a pattern
  of waves on the sand and says "home"
  to the drowsy pilgrim in a where-am-I? haze.

(After a three-hour wait I know my companion is
  on my list of people with whom it's OK to be stranded)

Short local hops don't, as might be supposed,
  come in small planes but at the tag end of jet flights
  from everywhere, exposing one to the accumulated
  frustrations of happy vacationers from London,
  Hawaii, you name it, discovering that the best place
  to visit is the one to which you return.

Found You, then, just once in the traditional way,
  but glimpsed you,
  maybe touched you now and then,
  all the time along the route.

NOTES ON CONTRIBUTORS

Biographical information on HORST BIENEK will be found in the note preceding his "Boyhood in Gleiwitz." EVA HESSE, the translator, edited the anthology *New Approaches to Ezra Pound: A Co-ordinated Investigation of Pound's Poetry and Ideas* (University of California, 1969).

A close friend and former literary agent and editor of the late Thomas Merton, NAOMI BURTON edited, with James Laughlin and Brother Patrick Hart, Merton's posthumous *Asian Journal*, appearing this year with New Directions.

FREDERICK BUSCH teaches literature at Colgate University. His novel, *I Wanted a Year without Fall*, was published in England in 1971, and a collection of stories, *Breathing Trouble*, in 1972. Recently, Syracuse University Press brought out his study of John Hawkes's fiction, *The Flesh Made Word*. Busch is now completing a new novel.

Born in Boston in 1924, CID CORMAN currently lives in Japan, where he edits and publishes the well-known literary magazine *Origin*. He has more than three dozen poetry collections to his credit, including *Livingdying* and *Sun Rock Man*, both brought out by New Directions in 1970. His "Eleven Poems" are part of a new volume, *o/1*, to be published this summer by the Elizabeth Press. An exhibition of Cormans' work was held this past winter at the Library of Brandeis University in Waltham, Massachusetts.

COLEMAN DOWELL, who was born in Kentucky, attended the University of the Philippines. He has worked as a composer-lyricist and written plays, one of which, *The Eve of the Green Grass*, was performed at the Chelsea Art Theatre with Kim Hunter in the lead. Random House brought out his first novel, *One of the Children Is Crying*, in 1968. He has since completed another novel, *Mrs. October Was Here*, and is, he says, "80% finished with a third," *Island People*, of which "The Keepsake" is a part.

ROBERT DUNCAN lives and works in San Francisco. *The Opening of the Field*, his first major poetry collection, was originally brought out in 1960, and is now being reissued as an ND Paperbook. New Directions also published two of Duncan's subsequent books, *Roots and Branches* (1964) and *Bending the Bow* (1968).

RUSSELL EDSON's *The Very Thing That Happens*, a book of fables illustrated with his own drawings, was published by New Directions in 1964. A short play, "Ketchup," was included in *ND23*, and an excerpt from an unpublished novel, *The Horsecock Chair*, appeared in *ND20*. His most recent books are *The Childhood of an Equestrian* (Harper & Row, 1972) and *The Clam Theater* (Wesleyan University Press, 1973).

DAVID GIANNINI has published a folder of six broadside poems, entitled *Opens*. With Richard Meyers, he was co-editor of *Genesis : Grasp* magazine and press. His poetry has appeared in *Baloney Street Magazine*, *ND23*, *Poems from the Hills*, *Quarterly Review of Literature*, and *Telephone*. Giannini was born in 1948 and now lives in Massachusetts.

Born in Pesaro, Italy, ALFREDO GIULIANI lives in Rome and holds a doctorate in philosophy. As a poet and critic, he is one of the most active representatives of the celebrated "Gruppo 63," and edited, with his fellow poet Nanni Balestrini, *I novissimi*, the seminal anthology of the Italian *neo-avant-garde*. He has translated into Italian poems by William Empson, James Joyce, Dylan Thomas, and surprisingly, Edwin Arlington Robinson. Giuliani's own poetry collections include *Il cuore zoppo* ("The Halting Heart"), *Povera Juliet e altre poesie* ("Poor Juliet and Other Poems"), and most recently, *Il Tautofono* ("The Tautophone"), from which the selection in this volume was taken. LUIGI BALLERINI teaches literature at the City College of the City University of New York. He has translated William Carlos William's *Kora in Hell* into Italian, published a book of his own poems, *eccetera. E.* (1972), and is now working on a study of the *neo-avant-garde* movement.

ANDREW GLAZE is a Southerner, born in Alabama, now living in New York. His first book of poems, *Damned Ugly Children* (Trident Press), was an "American Library Association Notable Book of 1966," and he taught at the Bread Loaf Writers' Conference at Middlebury College, Vermont, in 1969. Also a playwright, Glaze's *Kleinhoff Demonstrates Tonight* was produced earlier this year by Joseph Papp.

YUMIKO KURAHASHI's "The Ugly Devils" appeared last year in *ND24*, and since then she has published her second collection of essays, *Meiro no Tabibito* ("Travelers in the Labyrinth"). "Partei" was her first story, written while she was still attending Meiji University in Tokyo and launching her writing career. It was awarded a prize when it was printed in the student newspaper, and was later included as the title piece in a volume of short stories. The translators, SAMUEL GROLMES and his wife, YUMIKO TSUMURA, are now at work on the English version of Miss Kurahashi's novel *Yume no Ukihashi* ("The Floating Bridge of Dreams"), a modern treatment of themes from Lady Murasaki's 10th-century classic, *The Tale of Genji*.

ROBERT MORGAN was born in North Carolina in 1944, lived there until 1971, and now teaches in the writing program at Cornell University. His first book, *Zirconia Poems*, was published by Lillabulero in 1969; a new book, *Red Owl*, was brought out last year by W. W. Norton.

Among his various activities, ROBERT NICHOLS works as a landscape architect, building playgrounds on New York's Lower East Side. His plays have been performed by the Judson Poets' Theater and the Theater for the New City, and a volume of his verse, *Slow Newsreel of a Man Riding Train*, was brought out in 1961 by City Lights (Pocket Poet Series 16).

OMAR POUND teaches at the College of Arts and Technology in Cambridge, England, lecturing on anthropology and the Islamic world. His *Arabic and Persian Poems* was published by New Directions in 1970. Biographical information on OBEYD-I-ZAKANI will be found in the note preceding "Gorby and the Rats."

American by birth, DACHINE RAINER has been resident in Britain since 1961. She is the widow of the Scotsman E. J. Ballantine, sculptor, actor-director, and founder of the Provincetown Players, and is the mother of Thérèse Cantine, the ballet dancer. Miss

Rainer's poetry has been published in such magazines as *American Scholar, New Republic,* and *Quarterly Review of Literature,* and in a number of anthologies, including W. H. Auden's *The Criterion Book of Modern American Verse* (1956) and *ND12.* Her three-act drama, *Rembrant,* with music by Antonio Bibalo, is to have its world premiere in 1974.

KENNETH REXROTH lives in Santa Barbara, where he teaches at the University of California. Two of his recent books, published by Herder and Herder, are *The Alternative Society: Essays from the Other World* (1970) and *American Poetry: In the Twenieth Century* (1971), and last year Jonathan Cape brought out *The Rexroth Reader,* selected, with an introduction, by Eric Mottram. Ernesto Cardenal's "Coplas on the Death of Merton," translated by Rexroth and Mireya Jaime-Freyre, appeared in *ND25.*

The Greek poet YANNIS RITSOS was born in Monemvasia, in the Peloponnesos, in 1909. One of his country's most prolific writers, Ritsos' poems have been translated into as many as fourteen European languages and several of his shorter pieces set to music by Mikos Theodarakis. RAE DALVEN, whose rendering of Ritsos' "The Moonlight Sonata" appeared in *ND23,* is completing a volume of the poet's work, entitled *The Fourth Dimension.* For some recent translations of modern Greek poetry which were published in *Poetry* (August 1972) she was awarded the Jacob Glatstein Memorial Prize.

EDOUARD RODITI's *Magellan of the Pacific,* a biography of the Portuguese navigator, is being brought out this spring by Herder and Herder. "The Vampires of Istanbul," another of his Turkish tales, appeared in *ND24,* and a number of others have been published in *The Expatriate Review, The Literary Review,* and in *Playboy* as "Ribald Classics."

CLAUDIO RODRÍGUEZ, who presently teaches at the University of Madrid, is a country poet, born in 1934 in the Castilian town of Zamora. At eighteen, he wrote a seminal text in contemporary Spanish poetry, *Don de la ebriedad* ("The Gift of Inebriety," 1953), which portrayed the stark beauty of the Spanish countryside in language rich with peasant idioms. This was followed by *Conjuros*

("Conjurings," 1958), emphasizing his enchantment with village customs. Rodríguez's third book, *Alianza y condena* ("Alliance and Condemnation," 1965), from which the poems translated here were taken, was awarded the Premio de la Crítica. LOUIS M. BOURNE, who lives in Madrid, also translated "Ten Poems" of Carlos Bousoño, which appeared in *ND24*.

For the last three years, GARY SNYDER has lived with his family in the foothills of the Sierras in California. A leader in the ecology movement, he is working on a book for the Friends of the Earth. Recently, the Four Seasons Foundation brought out a small pamphlet of his new poems, entitled *Manzanita*. New Directions has published two volumes of his poetry, *The Back Country* (1968) and *Regarding Wave* (1970), and a prose collection, *Earth House Hold* (1969).

TONY TANNER, the author of *City of Words: American Fiction, 1950–1970* (Harper & Row, 1971), teaches at King's College, Cambridge. His essays and articles have appeared here and in Great Britain, in such periodicals as *Commentary*, *London Magazine*, the *New York Times*, the *Times Literary Supplement*, and the *New York Review of Books*.

CAROL TINKER, born in Pittsburgh, Pennsylvania, in 1940, grew up in New York, Japan, and Brandywine Hundred, Delaware, before attending Carnegie Mellon Institute. A painter as well as poet, she moved to San Francisco in 1962, traveled around the world in 1966–67, and now lives in Santa Barbara, California. Some of her work is included in the McGraw-Hill anthology *Four Young Women*, to be published this year.